1. Bed sheets are too small
2. Coffee? Food is only 'warm' never hot
3. Evaporated milk
4. No decen... ...e bars
5. Meths
6. Laxative ...oema...
   Take Kao...
7. Scorpions ...snakes
   Black widow spiders
   Jelly fish
8. Toilets — put paper in bins
9. Churches are locked due to icons being stolen.
10. Bingo, Hideous bars with space-invader machines & drunk tourists.
11. A disgusting omelette slouch tomcats. Mosquitos slate spinach pie fish v. expensive
12. Crowded beaches, people crammed in to sit where you are. Tacky tourist traps waiting
13. A shepherd with nasty habits. (120)

Lorna Chaplin first visited the Cyclades island of Paros in 1979 on a two week package holiday and fell in love with it at once. Return visits were limited while she completed her nursing training but Paros was her home from 1984 until she moved to the Peloponnese in 1989. The man who fixed the TV aerial is still there but they threw the television out years ago. The two original cats are hopefully enjoying Nirvana and their place is occupied by a homicidal feline and her brood. They have all been joined by the electrician's two children and are just waiting for Uncle Tom Cobbly!

To my husband Kostas Konstantinou
with all my love

About this book

The islands of Corfu and Paxos are fairly good examples of the two opposite extremes among Greek islands, both in regard to the degree of commercialisation and geographical size.

A large proportion of the visitors to Corfu in particular are there as part of a package holiday, and on the first evening the company representative will have given exhaustive information on local details and answered all questions. Many of the holiday complexes are so sophisticated that guests have no need to venture outside the grounds. This is why more detail has been given for Paxos and the smaller resorts and villages of Corfu not so involved in tourism; the aim is to provide the information needed when planning an itinerary of places to be visited by hired vehicle, public transport or on foot and generally making the most of your stay.

The language section is meant to help in emergencies only and is no substitute for a phrase book. Apart from place names, all Greek words in the text have been spelt phonetically in the way that produced the correct pronunciation during experiments!

This year has seen continuous price increases across the board and so the chances of the prices quoted here being accurate are nil. However the increases will be fairly uniform and so you can get an idea as to what to expect to pay.

Have a great time!

Acknowledgements

The author would like to thank Theodoros Varagoulis in Aghios Mattheos, Theodora Lindothoy in Sinarades, the mayor of Lefkimi, Angela Papageorgiou, Fotis for his veritable gold mine of information, Hellas Tours for their hospitality, and Grecofile of Halifax for their friendly assistance with addresses. Many thanks to John Fawssett for the information regarding travel by road to Greece; and to George, Spiridona and Thannasis of Corfu Sun Motors for keeping my bike on the road against all the odds.

Front Cover: *Not wishing to break with what has become almost a tradition, we have used this view of what has become a symbol of Corfu — Pontikonissi and Vlacherna islets — for our cover.* P. 73

Greek Island Series

Corfu,
Paxos and Antipaxos

Lorna Chaplin

Roger Lascelles, Cartographic and Travel Publisher
47 York Road, Brentford, Middlesex TW8 OQP. Tel: 081-847 0935

Publication Data

Title	Corfu, Paxos and Antipaxos
Typeface	Phototypeset in Compugraphic Times
Photographs	Lorna Chaplin (unless otherwise stated)
Maps	Joyplan, Chessington, Surrey.
Index	Jane Thomas
Printing	Kelso Graphics, Kelso, Scotland.
ISBN	0 903909 94 4
Edition	This first, Feb 1992
Publisher	Roger Lascelles
	47 York Road, Brentford, Middlesex, TW8 0QP.
Copyright	Lorna Chaplin

Distribution

Africa:	South Africa	Faradawn, Box 17161, Hillbrow 2038
Americas:	Canada	International Travel Maps & Books, P.O. Box 2290, Vancouver BC V6B 3W5
	U.S.A.	Available through major booksellers with good foreign travel sections.
Asia:	India	English Book Store, 17-L Connaught Circus, P.O. Box 328, New Delhi 110 001
Australasia	Australia	Rex Publications, 15 Huntingdon Street, Crows nest, N.S.W.
Europe:	Belgium	Brussels — Peuples et Continents
	Germany	Available through major booksellers with good foreign travel sections
	GB/Ireland	Available through all booksellers with good foreign travel sections.
	Italy	Libreria dell'Automobile, Milano
	Netherlands	Nilsson & Lamm BV, Weesp
	Denmark	Copenhagen — Arnold Busck, G.E.C. Gad, Boghallen
	Finland	Helsinki — Akateeminen Kirjakauppa
	Norway	Oslo — Arne Gimnes/J.G. Tanum
	Sweden	Stockholm/Esselte, Akademi Bokhandel, Fritzes, Hedengrens. Gothenburg/Gumperts, Esselte. Lund/Gleerupska
	Switzerland	Basel/Bider: Berne/Atlas; Geneve/Artou; Lausanne/Artou: Zurich/Travel Bookshop

Contents

Part 1: Planning Your Holiday

Part 2: Corfu, Paxos and Antipaxos

Appendices

Index

ONE

Introducing the Greek Islands

No matter where you live in Britain, whether it be in a depressingly grim industrial area or a quaint rural village, the Greek islands are so different, so "un-British". There are islands where it is possible to imagine an advertising company having designed every feature in such a style as would make it most appealing to visitors. Tiny white sugar cubes have shutters and doors painted all the colours of the rainbow side by side with flaming geraniums and bougainvilia to make the brightest display. There's higgledy piggledy town planning with mazes of winding streets containing picture postcard court-yards and balconies; grey flagstones with the joins painstakingly whitewashed and here and there a magnificent forsythia or clematis springing from the tiniest cracks between them; harbours and shorelines dotted with little fishing boats lovingly painted in the most brilliant colours by their proud owners, who can be seen at sunset tenderising octopus on the rocks before hanging them up to dry.

The street displays of the shops rival that of any Eastern bazaar and the cries can be heard of the traders who peddle fruit, vegetables and fish from baskets attached to the saddles of enigmatic looking donkeys; road traffic consists of octogenarians riding donkeys and mules, overtaken by the ever-so-slightly faster drivers of rotovator engines attached to their two wheeled carts.

Fields of impossibly red poppies and sunkissed daisies inspire even those who have never before looked twice at a wild flower; here are rolling hills, rocky mountains with a house, chapel or monastery gouged seemingly inaccessibly into them; dry stone walls, ramshackle farm buildings, goitre-necked cattle, indignant turkeys, skittish sheep and vociferous farm dogs.

The pace of life and attitude to it are summarised by the custom of asking anyone seen looking at their watch if they are taking antibiotics. What other reason could you have for needing to know what time it is!

A statue of one of the famous Theotoki family in King George's Square, where the Ionian Bank branch that houses the paper money museum and Aghios Spiridonas church are located.

How fresh seems the enthusiasm on the faces of the dancers who are lured to the floor by the bazouki music, like sailors to the sirens; the generosity and hospitality of anyone whose threshhold you cross. How the conversations full of shouting and gesticulating contrast with the unearthly quiet of siesta time. Get the picture? It is just gloriously different!

The Ionian Islands

The Ionian Islands are known to the Greeks as "Ta Eptanissia": the seven islands comprise Corfu, Paxos, Levkas, Kefallonia, Ithaka, Zakynthos and Kythira. The latter, far to the south, is generally grouped with the Ionians although it is not located in the Ionian sea.

Each island has its own individual character but the Ionian islands as a whole differ from the mainland and other island groups owing to their geographical position, which has affected them in two ways. Firstly, as seems to have been evident to many strategists seeking to have control of the Mediterranean and the adjoining lands, the islands were an ideal and necessary base from which to pursue conquests and monopolise trade routes. This resulted in their being under the occupancy of a succession of foreign masters, most notably the Venetians whose 400 years inevitably left a deep impression on the islands; and it is an indication of their deep sense of national identity that during this time they maintained their own religion, language and, to a large extent, culture.

The second geographical role is perhaps more meteorological as their extreme north westerly position gives rise to lower temperature and considerably higher rainfall. This, together with a sponsored tree planting scheme by the Venetians, has resulted in the rich green cloak that the islands wear, which is in sharp contrast to the deforested hills just visible on the mainland. Like the countryside, the architecture of the towns and villages has a distinctly Italian flavour, with some British influence here and there from our fifty-year occupation which saw the beginning of the British fascination with these islands that is still evident today.

Corfu

Corfu (Kerkyra) is a very unusual if not unique island that contains all aspects of Greek life, from the black clad figure of a peasant woman riding her donkey side saddle home from the vinyards at the end of the day to the casino in the palace. The ultra simple and the ultra sophisticated are all here. Olive groves that completely cover the mountain slopes make this a green and pleasant land. The Venetian architecture of the city wears better than traditional British or Greek styles and there is nothing but charm in the town area.

Paxos

Beautifully Greek with just a hint of the Venetian, this little island is a cool olive grove edged with tiny coves, awe inspiring cliffs, come hither sea and delightful fishing villages. For the Greek experience and a relaxing get-away-from-it-all holiday there is no better choice of destination.

Antipaxos

Although the population is theoretically over a hundred, the few who stay overnight on what is generally a day trip destination will have to look a long way for company. What the landscape lacks is made up for in the beauty of the famous beaches.

Tourist information

The National Tourist Office of Greece

(NTOG) Known in Greece as EOT (pronounced like yacht), this organisation is generally helpful and friendly. The British branch is at 195/197 Regent Street, London W1R 8DR. Nearest underground stations Oxford Circus and Piccadilly Circus.

NTOG produce two pamphlets relevant to the islands in this book. The fourteen-page *The Ionian islands* and the eight-page *Corfu* contain a list of hotels, some colour photographs, brief details of places to see and in the case of the latter, a useful street map of the town.

Offices on the Greek mainland that you might find useful are:

● Patras: 110 Iroon Polytekniou and Stathmos B, port buildings;
● Pireaus: Marina Zeas;
● Athens: East main airport, Elliniko; National Bank of Greece,
1 Karageorgi Servias Street and Syntagma Square; General Bank of
Greece, 1 Ermou Street and Syntagma Square. Offices are generally
open Monday to Friday 08.00 to 20.00hrs and 09.00 to 13.00 on
Saturdays; closed Sundays.

The Iroon Polytekniou office in Patras is purely administrative
and enquiries should be made of one of the grumpy women in the
office at the entrance to the port buildings.

Tourist police
There used to be a separate tourist police force equipped with
armbands bearing the flags of the countries whose language they
spoke. Although signs marked 'Tourist Police Station' are still the
thing to look for, these are mostly now within the regular police
offices where an officer is available to deal with any complaints or
queries and dispense leaflets and maps to visitors. Some of them
even speak a language other than Greek!

Policemen are not allowed to work in their home towns and their
postings are changed every two years, so they won't have as much
personal knowledge of the area as one of the locals.

Passports
Visitors to Greece require a valid passport which may be the British
Visitor's Passport issued by post offices in the UK. Entry may be
refused to anyone whose passport contains the stamp of a Turkish
Cypriot port. Nationals of non-EEC countries should check with
the Greek embassy as to visa requirements.

Passports are no longer stamped on entry or exit but the visa
regulations for those wishing to stay beyond the three months that
the non existent "stamp" entitles are the same as ever; these require
five passport photographs, proof of funds other than cash (they get
fed up with seeing the same old bank notes pooled amongst friends),
pink slips from the bank or other proof that you have exchanged
foreign currency since your arrival, a completed form from a notary
public with details of just about everything including where your
granny had her birth mark, an assortment of stamps (without which
nothing is ever valid in Greece) and a lot of hanging about looking
humble.

TWO

When to go

It doesn't seem safe anymore to make generalisations about the climate as our poor old planet appears to be going through some fairly dramatic changes; in Greece, as in Britain, no one can remember the weather ever being this hot/cold/dry so early/late and the seasons seem to have been changed around.

Rainfall

A problem that everyone is aware of is the diminished amount of rain, which means that the shortages and cuts in the water supply start earlier each year; and although no one would wish for constant rain on their holiday, it means that those going to Paxos will have to put up with rationing of the fresh water supplies.

When you look at Corfu and Paxos from a distance, the amount of rich vegetation must warn you that they do get a fair amount of rain, and indeed Corfu gets nearly as much as London. The staggering difference is between the weather on Corfu and Paxos when you consider that they are only 7km apart. Comparing the number of days of rain during my stay on Corfu with what the locals on Paxos experienced during the same period, I found that Paxos had only a tenth of the number of days of rain; what on Corfu had been a downpour amounted to no more than a drizzle on Paxos.

The table gives some statistics from the days when things were more stable, to let you get some idea of the average weather conditions.

Average weather conditions, Corfu

Average monthly wind speed and direction

Jan	Feb	Mar	Apr	May	Jun	Jul	Aug	Sep	Oct	Nov	Dec
SE	SE	SE	SE	W	W	NW	NW	SE	SE	SE	SE
			2.9	2.6	2.9	2.9	2.6	2.3	2.6		

Average air temperatures °C

Jan	Feb	Mar	Apr	May	Jun	Jul	Aug	Sep	Oct	Nov	Dec
10.1	10.4	12.1	15.3	19.7	24.0	26.6	26.5	22.9	18.7	14.9	11.6

Average sea temperature °C at surface 14.00hrs

Jan	Feb	Mar	Apr	May	Jun	Jul	Aug	Sep	Oct	Nov	Dec
13.8	13.6	14.0	16.0	19.3	22.0	24.0	24.8	24.0	20.7	17.8	15.0

Average number of rainy days

Jan	Feb	Mar	Apr	May	Jun	Jul	Aug	Sep	Oct	Nov	Dec
16.9	14.7	14.8	11.9	9.3	5.0	2.0	3.1	7.3	12.5	16.5	18.4

Average daily hours of sunshine

Jan	Feb	Mar	Apr	May	Jun	Jul	Aug	Sep	Oct	Nov	Dec
5	6	7	7	9	10	11	12	9	6	4	3

Temperature

Don't be put of by those news items of people dropping like flies in Athens owing to the heat. Athens becomes stifling because of the *néfos* pollution cloud that hangs permanently over the city, and on bad days you start choking before your ferry docks in Piraeus. While this is worth bearing in mind if you are planning to spend time in the capital during July and August, the conditions are vastly different on the islands and most mainland areas.

At the same time, it is the amount of humidity in the air that determines whether the temperatures are nicely hot or sloth inducingly sticky, and you don't get all that forest without some humidity. A lightweight waterproof jacket or what used to be called a plastic mac will at least mean that you have a means of getting from your accommodation to a restaurant without getting soaked, should you be unlucky enough to get a rainy day — because when it rains on Corfu it really rains! After such spells the air feels as if it has been given a spring clean. That slight haze that hangs over the hills has disappeared for a few hours and keen photographers dash out and get their shots of the Albanian hills and mountain ranges.

A thin cardigan or jacket is an idea for the evenings as it can feel chilly after sunset, especially when your goose bumps are sun burnt!

Winds

The locals are always aware of which wind is blowing and usually have a pretty good idea of which will be blowing tomorrow. The most common visitor is the Maestros from the north west followed by the Ostria, a less refreshing current of air from the south. The much despised Sirocco has an almost unearthly quality, as its effects are the subject of legend and judges take into account crimes committed after a few days of this noisy southeasterly wind that makes everyone irritable.

Late April to mid June and mid September to mid October are the best months for holidays, with the earlier season having the advantage of the brilliant displays of spring flowers, the like of which is only seen in the fields of mustard and rape at home, while the autumn visitors have the advantage of warmer seas.

THREE

Getting to the Greek mainland

Direct flights to Corfu

The quickest and undoubtedly the cheapest way of travelling from the UK to Corfu and Paxos is to fly direct to Corfu. With the holiday firms suffering from the drop in public spending, the competition is intense and prices for package holidays, especially the late savers, reach a level where they are cheaper than a flight only deal, certainly by the scheduled routes which, of course, don't have the benefit of accommodation.

Even if you don't wish to spend all your time at a resort, the convenience of the inexpensive travel, door-to-door service and the use of the accommodation whenever you choose, make this an option to consider.

In addition to the well known companies that block book complete hotels in the resort areas, there are some smaller, often local companies who still have enough of the personal touch to offer villa holidays and hotel accommodation at the quieter villages. Here are brief details of those whose name plates I have noticed on gate posts; your travel agent is unlikely to have heard of them:

Corfu a La Carte 8 Deenwood House, Stockcross, Newbury, Berks RG16 8JP.
CV Travel 43 Cadogen Street, Chelsea, London SW3 2PR. Corfu and Paxos (including luxury standard) villa holidays.
Starvillas 25 High Street, Chesterton, Cambs CB4 1ND. Corfu villa holidays.
Timsway Holidays Nightingales Corner, Little Chalfont, Bucks HP7 9QS. Corfu and Paxos hotel holidays.
Something Special 10 Bull Plain, Hertford SG14 1DT. Corfu villa holidays.
Leisure Villas 21 Palmerstone Road, London SW19 1PG.
Corfu and Paxos villa holidays.

Loggos Tours Ltd 51 High Street, Newport, Gwent NP9 1GB. Paxos and Antipaxos villa holidays.
Routsis Holidays 1 Timsworth Close, Luton, Beds LU2 9SF. Paxos villa, sailing and watersports holidays.
Planos Holidays 31 Gladstone Road, Combedown, Bath BA2 5HL. Paxos hotel, villa and apartment holidays.
Greek Islands Club 66 High Street, Walton-on-Thames, Surrey KT12 1BV. Paxos villa, apartments, sailing and windsurfing.

A most helpful agency are **Grecofile** (telephone Halifax 0422 310201), who specialise in finding a package holiday tailor-made to your specific requirements.

Flight only details are available from your local travel agent or from the agencies listed in the low price travel magazines and entertainment guides sold in large newsagents.

To enter Greece in this way, regulations demand that you have an accommodation voucher. The companies that sell flight only seats will provide you with such a voucher for a token payment of a few pounds. When you receive your tickets the wallet will also include a confirmation of booking at an address within the mainland or Corfu. You are not expected to use this address and could find that it is a derelict building if you try to do so.

A similar fiction works in the case of booking an outward only flight, when bogus return flight details will be inserted in the appropriate spaces on the ticket. It is illegal for the charter companies to sell seats in Greece and so the aircraft often have empty seats that would be snapped up if they were on sale. The Athens press often carry personal advertisements for flights to British airports and nine times out of ten they turn out to be for these non existent flights either with or without the seller being aware of it.

Scheduled flights direct to Kerkyra arrive once per week each from Amsterdam, Dusseldorf, Frankfurt, Geneva, London, Milan, Rome and Stuttgart. With the charter flights the number of arrivals peaked at fifty five per day on occasions last year.

By air to Athens

The country's main airport is in Athens and although there is a second airport in Thessaloniki to the north, it is unlikely that any of you would want to use the weekly flight there from London, as it is much farther away from the islands and their departure points.

The airport is situated ten kilometres south of the centre of Athens and the main buildings are divided into what are known as the east main airport and the west main airport — but both use the same runways. The west main airport is used exclusively by Olympic Airways, the Greek national airline, for both overseas and domestic flights. The east main airport is used by all airlines except Olympic

There are daily flights to Athens with an average flight time of 3½ hours from the following British airports: Aberdeen, Belfast, Birmingham, Bristol, Edinburgh, Glasgow, Leeds, Liverpool, Manchester, Newcastle, Norwich, Southampton and, of course, the three London airports.

By rail to the Greek mainland

Greece is connected by rail to almost every European country including Finland, USSR and Turkey. Within Greece trains proceed extremely slowly with long and frequent stops at stations which for some reason aren't taken into account on the local timetables and trains are therefore notoriously late.

From England the cost is suprisingly high and greatly exceeds that of the average budget flight even for those under 26 years of age or who hold a student card. There are daily departures from London's Victoria Station for Athens. A typical journey departs 14.30 hrs Monday and arrives at 07.30 on Thursday, with changes of train in Paris and Venice. Under 26's are eligible for the Eurorail card that entitles you to unlimited travel on any of Europe's railways for one month.

International arrivals by rail are to the Peloponnisos station and departures for Patras, the mainland port of departure to Corfu and Paxos, are also from there. However if you are journeying to Athens from elsewhere in Greece, your arrival may be at the Larissis station.

The two railway stations of Peloponnisos and Larissis are only 200m away from each other on foot and are linked by a bridge — which unfortunately means you have to climb a large number of steps. By road, however, it is quite a different story. Owing to the boundary walls, tracks and one-way system, a taxi ride from one station to the other can seem as if you have travelled from one town to another; but is unlikely to exceed the minimum fare plus the allowance charged for picking up from a station and dropping off at a station.

I have heard many tales of long delays at the borders for rail passengers and of harassment by customs officials. Except for Eurorail card users, it would seem that the only advantage in this form of transport is for those who hate flying.

You can get to both stations by public transport:

● From the airport, Express Bus B and Ḃ.
● From KTEL Kifisou, Express Bus A or Ȧ and change to B or Ḃ
● From Piraeus, Elektrikos train to Omonia and then by Green Bus no. 040 or trolley no. 1 from Voulis Street.

By coach to the Greek mainland

Well, things have at last improved in this the cheapest way of reaching Greece, with the return coach fare costing considerably less than the 2nd class rail single. The disaster stories of the past now sound like pioneers' adventure yarns but if you made the trip in "the bad old days", it is still difficult to have faith in the inevitability of your arrival!

The Greek rail company's coaches (yes — that's right!) are of the luxury variety where you sit on the top above the heads of the driver and his mate who have a cabin to use for their sleep breaks. There is a toilet and wash basin — though they never work and will be locked for the duration of the trip; but as there are regular stops for you to use the loos there is no problem unless you don't happen to carry the right coins to stick in the slots in six different countries!

Food is still forbidden on board which is no inconvenience as the refreshment stops offer a wide range of food (omelette only in Yugoslavia) and you can get an excellent three course meal for the approximate cost of the London to Athens air fare!

Departures are twice weekly to the Peloponnisos railway station and a typical journey leaves London at 14.30 on Tuesday and reaches Athens at 09.00hrs on Friday but the buses are fast. (On the return journey I and the other three passengers with tickets to continue from Brussels to London, faced a wait of 12 hours before the departure for the last leg of the journey. We all opted to buy tickets for the "City Sprint" service that crossed via hovercraft from Calais and we were in London at 16.00hrs rather than late morning the following day, as was the schedule with the original carrier.)

Arriving in Athens the driver will stop at Syntagma Square and the home of that little old lady who is friendly with his mother-in-law, before the end of the line at the mainline railway stations.

> **A nasty moment!**
> Waiting outside the coach for the driver to do us the honour of letting
> us on, I spotted the wording on the cover of the ticket of one of my
> fellow travellers and scenes from all those past nightmare journeys
> flashed before me; it read "Magic Bus".

By road to the Greek mainland

The distance between London and Athens is 3,250km or 2,000 miles
and this poses the only major difficulty in the journey. My Europe-
hopping colleague John Fawssett informs me that the best route is
via Austria and using the new motorway from Salzburg to
Klagenfurt and on to the M1/E94-E5 from Ljubljana in Yugoslavia.
An alternative route is through Italy to one of the ports which has
ferry services to Greece — such as Ancona, Bari, Brindisi.

The standard of the major road network used in passing through
Italy contrasts sharply with that in Yugoslavia. While the Italian
Autostrade is one of the best in Europe, the main route through
Yugoslavia is largely along single carriageway roads or, worse still,
the deadly three lane system where the middle lane is used for
overtaking by vehicles going in both directions. The sides of the
roads are littered with recent wrecks and the flatness of the
surrounding landscape does little to help the driver ward off sleep.
A difficult stretch of road north of Belgrade can be avoided by
taking the M3 from Maribor via Osijek to Srem.

The AA can supply routes for both members and non-members.
The routes are individually prepared — you tell them through which
countries and towns you wish to pass and they can then either
provide the AA recommended route or a customised route. On
customised routes, travellers can specify whether they wish to take
the scenic route, the fastest route, avoid motorways etc. Routes can
be purchased from the AA Overseas Routes Unit, Danum House,
Basingstoke, Hants RG21 2EA.

Petrol coupons

In Italy a complicated system of petrol coupons exists to offset the
deterrent to tourism of current prices, which are among the most
expensive in Europe. The most useful of the four packages for those
passing through Italy purely to catch a ferry to Corfu or Patras is
the "Pachetto Otalia", which provides you with 12 coupons each

worth 11 litres that can be used at major petrol stations throughout the country.

The best way of obtaining these is to get them from the ACI offices at border crossing points, where any unused coupons can be redeemed. Free motorway toll vouchers are supplied with these coupons to present when leaving the motorway network together with the ticket that was issued on your entry to the road.

It is no longer compulsory for visitors to Yugoslavia to buy petrol coupons at the borders (from the AMSJ); the five per cent saving that they offered was often retained by the attendants.

Greece has no petrol coupon system at the present time.

Greek fuel prices

The way these have been increasing lately, there isn't much chance of these figures being correct by the time I finish typing this paragraph! Currently super is 150drs, regular 140drs and diesel 90drs per litre.

There are now so many unleaded petrol supplies in smog bound Greece that no list exists any more.

Speed limits and regulations

In Italy speed limits are usually 110km/h on all main roads, but in an effort to reduce the amount of accidents at weekends, the limit decreases to 90km/h. Visitors are not immune to the on-the-spot fines imposed by traffic policemen.

In Greece, the maximum speed is 100km/h, which is quite fast enough on roads that often have unmarked pot-holes and bumps.

Drivers going into Greece should be aware of the following regulations:

● If the level of alcohol in their bloodstream is between 0.05% and 0.08% it is a civil offence, more than 0.08% is a criminal offence.

● Police can impose fines, but not collect them on-the-spot. The fine must be paid at the Public Treasury office within 10 days. Drivers can be fined for unnecessary use of their car horn.

● Children under 10 are not permitted to travel in a vehicle as front seat passengers. Seat belts are compulsory for both driver and front seat passenger.

● Drivers must carry a fire extinguisher, first-aid kit and warning triangle. It is forbidden to carry petrol in a can in a vehicle.

Documentation and spares

Driving licence, car registration documents and your green insurance card should be presented at the various borders and on request. At the Greek border, the customs official will complete a form that contains your details and those of the vehicle — a measure that is designed to prevent your selling it within the country at a great profit (for the price of an ancient MOT failure in Greece you could buy one of the new inexpensive makes in Britain). The counterfoil must be kept to hand over when you exit from Greece.

Your car should be properly serviced before embarking on a long journey. The AA recommends drivers to take a spare clutch cable, since right hand drive cables are a different length from left hand drive, and there could be a delay in receiving a cable to fit the car.

By ship to Corfu

Most of the international ferries that sail between Italy or Yugoslavia and Patras or Igoumenitsa in Greece call at Corfu, linking the island with the following ports:

From		duration	frequency
Italy	Ancona	22hrs	daily
	Bari	11	every 3 days
	Brindisi	10	3 per day
Yugoslavia	Dubrovnik	11	2 per week

By ship to the Greek mainland

In the list that follows, the entries that are noted as being of seldom frequency are those of the Black Sea Shipping Company, a Russian cruise line whose itinerary indirectly links Piraeus with the ports of most European countries.

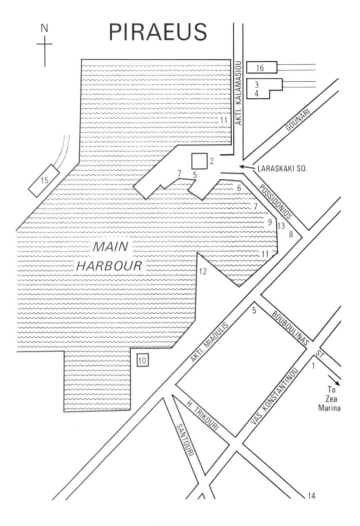

PIRAEUS

N

16

3
4

GOUNARI

AKTI. KALAMASIOU

11

2

15

7   5

← LARASKAKI SQ.

6

7

POSSIDONIOS

9   13

8

MAIN
HARBOUR

11

12

5

BOUBOULINAS

10

AKTI. MIAOULIS

ST.

1

VAS. KONSTANTINOU

To
Zea
Marina

H. TRIKOURI

SANTOURI

14

Places of Interest

1. Athens Bus
2. Bus Terminal
3. Chondrocousis Travel Office
4. Elektrikos Train
5. Express Bus No 19 stops
6. Car Ferries to Aegina & Poros
7. Passenger Ferries to Saronic Gulf
8. Information Office (Summer)
9. Small Ferries to Aegina, Angistri & Salamis
10. Customs Hall
11. Aegean Islands Ferries
12. International Ferries
13. Port Authority Control Desk
14. Flying Dolphin Booking Office
15. Train Station to Northern Greece
16. Train Station to Peloponnese

From	between	duration	frequency
Cyprus	Larnaka-Piraeus	40½hrs	weekly
	Limassol-Piraeus	45	weekly
Egypt	Alexandria-Piraeus	22	every 10 days
France	Marseille-Piraeus	86	seldom
Israel	Haifa-Piraeus	62	2/week
Italy	Ancona-Igoumenitsa	23	3 daily
	Ancona-Patras	34	3 daily
	Bari-Igoumentitsa	12½	every 3 days
	Bari-Patras	22	daily
	Brindisi-Igoumenitsa	11	3 daily
	Brindisi-Patras	20	2 daily
	Genoa-Piraeus	68	seldom
	Naples-Piraeus	43	seldom
	Venice-Piraeus	50	every 10 days
Russia	Odessa-Piraeus	55	weekly
Syria	Lattakia-Piraeus	46	weekly
Turkey	Kusadasi-Piraeus	15½	weekly
	Izmir-Piraeus	n.a.	weekly
Yugoslavia	Dubrovnik-Patras	22½	2/week
	Dubrovnik-Piraeus	27	every 10 days
	Rijeka-Igoumenitsa	39	weekly
	Split-Patras	25	weekly

Piraeus

Greece's main port is easily reached from both the centre of Athens and the airport.
● From the airports, Express Bus no. 19.
● From central Athens, *elektrikos* from Omonia or Monastiraki, Green Bus no. 040 from Fillelinon Street off Syntagma Square.
● From the rail stations, trolley bus no. 1 to Amalias or Voulis in central Athens and then as above.
● From KTEL Kifisou bus station, Express Bus A or ⅄ to Syntagma Square in central Athens, then as above.

Not suprisingly, the port is not a very attractive area and the overall impression is of "grey" despite the presence of some new port buildings which have been recently completed in the struggle to improve facilities at what is a grossly over crowded port.

The National Tourist Organisation of Greece prints a free weekly sailing timetable for all ports which can be obtained from any of their offices. Most daily newspapers print a list of the day's departures, but in Greek, of course. For port police information tel. (01) 451 1311 and 417 2657 and for a recorded timetable of the day's departures in Greek and English tel. 143.

Because of the size of the port, it is essential to know where your ferry leaves from. Ask when buying your ticket and confirm it at the tourist police office just inside the *elektrikos* station. The Chondrocoucis travel office just inside the station is the only one I have found that really does sell tickets for all the companies and therefore supplies accurate information regarding the first departure. etc.

Along the main road parallel to the dock, are banks, souvenir shops, cafés, tavernas, trolley and bus stops and the entrance to the *elektrikos* station. Within the port area there is now a 24 hour snack bar.

FOUR

Corfu and Paxos
from mainland Greece

The previous chapter should have given you enough information to have got yourselves either directly to Corfu or somewhere on the Greek mainland. This chapter aims to explain the alternatives available for the completion of the journey to Corfu and Paxos and to provide some useful information for those that will want to visit other islands.

Having reached the mainland it is necessary to decide which method you intend to use for the last leg of the journey. Because both destinations are islands, either an air or sea crossing is, of course, inevitable. This means that a number of crossing points exist plus a variety of ways of reaching them from where ever you happen to be on the mainland. Mainland departure points are:
- For Corfu
  West main airport, Patras and Igoumenitsa.
- For Paxos
  Patras, Igoumenitsa, Parga and Mourtos.

By air from Athens

Departures are from the west main airport. It is usually necessary to make a reservation as the flights soon become full. Travel agents in the UK can make the booking for you. When choosing which flight to take, don't forget to take into account your possible late arrival from the previous leg, and also the transfer time involved in getting to the west main airport terminal which, even from the east main airport, can take over an hour.
- From east main airport, Olympic airways shuttle bus, hourly departures. Express Bus no. 19.
- From central Athens, Express A and B; Bus no.133 from Othonos Street in Syntagma Square from 05.40 to 24.00hrs every 20 minutes, fare 40drs; Bus no.122 from Vas. Olgas Avenue 05.30 to

The mainland port of Igoumenitsa seen from the upper deck of one of the many car ferries that make the two-hour crossing to Kerkyra.

23.30hrs every 15 minutes, fare 40drs; Night bus no. 167 from Academias Street off Syntagma Square approximately hourly from 00.30 to 04.00hrs.
- From Piraeus, Express Bus no. 19.
- From KTEL Kifisou Bus Terminal, Express Bus A.
- From railway stations, Express Bus B.

There are three or four daily flights from Athens that use the 146-seater 727 aircraft for the fifty-minute journey. Single fare 9,700drs.

On Wednesdays and Saturdays a nineteen-seater Dornier connects Corfu with Kefallonia, Preveza and Zakynthos, so these are also possible departure points.

Via Patras

This, the fourth largest Greek town, is a busy port for both passenger and freight transport to and from Italy and Yugoslavia. The NTOG print an excellent street map of this grid system town which deserves some exploration; but for those with little time to spare, Patras is conveniently laid out and the port, railway station and bus depot are all located within 400m of each other.

Like most ports, poor old Patras is overworked and undersized. Although new facilities have been added they were inadequate before their completion. The dock area is divided into two sections with the usual facilities at both ends. To the south (your left when facing the sea) is Stathmos A, the original buildings which for the purposes of this book deal only with the vessels of Karageorgis and Venturis lines which dock there. While there is a large duty free shop, the facilities are not as extensive as at Stathmos B, where there is a small NTOG office, exchange desk, OTE, bar, snack bar and waiting area. The vessels of all the other companies leave via this area of the dock which is signposted from the outskirts of Patras onwards — although when leaving the town the route to Athens is not at all clear.

Some 200m before the bus depot the road crosses the rail tracks and becomes a one-way system on its way to the railway station, opposite the pleasant if expensive cafés of the Trion Simahon Square. Here are two kiosks with a large selection of English language books, papers and magazines and the main branch of the National Bank of Greece which, in addition to the usual opening hours, is open for exchange purposes each evening from 17.30 to 20.00 and at weekends from 11.00 to 13.00. This area has a handful of hotels ranging from the luxury to the disreputable.

The main (and nearest) post office is best found by walking through the bus station and continuing along the narrow streets without turning until you have crossed two major roads and are facing the third, at which time the post office will be directly on your left. Open from 07.30 to 20.00 Monday to Friday and 08.00 to 13.30 on Saturdays. The Poste Restante is on the right as you enter and may only be open until 10.00hrs.

Turning right out of the post office you soon come to Platea Olgas with shaded cafés and benches. On the first corner is the museum. Continuing in a staight line you come to the third and largest of the town's squares which offers no shade around its fountains. Here is a large one-hour photograph developing shop and many chemists.

The most comprehensive way of detailing the bewildering array of routes out of Patras is to list them under the individual shipping companies. Competition amongst them is fairly intense but this isn't something that will bother the average passenger who is likely to decide which vessel to take by the departure time and, if continuing on from Corfu, the subsequent destinations of the route.

There is a regulation (that will soon be quashed by the EEC) that only Greek-owned ships may transport passengers between two Greek ports. So if you wish to use one of the vessels of the Italian or Yugoslavian lines and won't be continuing your journey with the same company to another country, you must apply for a permit from the port police. Your travel agent will give you the details of how this is done but it means that you should allow extra time.

- **Adriatika** (Italian owned) Patras, Igoumenitsa, Corfu, Brindisi. Daily.
- **Anek** Patras, Igoumenitsa, Corfu, Ancona. Daily.
- **Fragline** Patras, Igoumenitsa, Corfu, Brindisi. Daily.
- **H.M.L.** Patras, Igoumenitsa, Corfu, Brindisi. Daily.
- **Minoan** Patras, Igoumenitsa, Corfu, Ancona. 5 per week.
- **Seven Islands** The company runs two routes on alternate days. Day 1: Patras, Kefallonia, Ithaki, Paxos, Igoumenitsa, Corfu, Brindisi. Day 2: Patras, Igoumenitsa, Corfu, Brindisi.
- **Strinzis** Patras, Igoumenitsa, Corfu, Ancona. Daily except Sunday.
- **Ventouris** Patras, Igoumenitsa, Corfu, Bari. Daily.

Getting to Patras
Getting to Patras from Athens or Piraeus is not a problem but you need to leave yourself enough time. All the above mentioned shipping companies have coaches from Piraeus via the centre of Athens to Patras, fare 1,500drs. In addition:
- KTEL bus from the 100 Kifisou terminus. From 06.30 to 21.30 approximately hourly. Journey time 3½ hours. Fare 1,550drs.
- OSE bus from Peloponnisos railway station. From 05.40 to 21.30 at least hourly. Journey time 3 hours. Fare 1,550drs.
- OSE train from Peloponnisos railway station. From 06.25 to 21.41, 7 daily departures. Journey time 4½ hours (+ !). Fare 1,100drs 1st class, 730drs 2nd class.

Via Igoumenitsa

Located just under a hundred kilometres from Ioannina, this is a much smaller port and town than Patras. The most noticeable feature is the modern looking prefecture building whose gay colour scheme belies the fact that it is one of the oldest buildings in the town. The bus station is a full kilometre north of the port and many ticket offices and a National Bank are passed en route.

Routes from Igoumenitsa are:

● To Kerkyra, 10 daily departures between 05.00 and 22.00hrs. Two hour journey. Fare 500drs. Car ferry.

● To Paxos, Mondays, Wednesdays and Fridays 10.00hrs. Two hour journey. Fare 500drs. Car ferry.

Getting to Igoumenitsa
From Athens take the KTEL bus from 100 Kifisou terminus. Departures at 06.30, 12.00 and 19.15. Journey time 8 hours. Fare 3,400drs.

Via Parga

Fifty kilometres south of Igoumenitsa lies Parga. The area around this little port is attractive enough to have made it a popular resort. Long lonely stretches of pebbly beach backed by thickly wooded hills provide the landscape of the region.

From Parga there are daily departures to Paxos at 09.00hrs on what is really an excursion trip that takes passengers only. Journey time 1 hour.

Getting to Parga
From Athens take the KTEL bus to Preveza from 100 Kifisou terminus. Departures at 07.00, 13.30 and 20.00hrs. Journey time 7 hours. Fare 3,000drs. You then take the local bus to Parga.

Via Mourtos (Sivota)

A short hop (twenty kilometres south) from Igoumenitsa is this
small resort, shown on the maps as Sivota but known by the local
people as Mourtos. From Mourtos there are departures to Paxos,
Tuesdays and Thursdays at 07.30hrs; but check departure details
with the port police.

Private transport

Those arriving in Greece by means of their own transport will have
done so in one of two ways, either by having driven across the
border into northern Greece or aboard one of the car ferries. In
both cases the place to head for is Igoumenitsa to make the crossing
to Corfu or Paxos.

Island hopping possibilities

The Ionian Islands offer within the group islands of all types,
ranging from highly commercialised and exclusive to simple and
almost uninhabited. The volume entitled *Kefallonia and the South
Ionian Islands* in this series gives invaluable information on
Kefallonia, Ithaka, Levkas and Zakinthos while Kythira is
considered in the volume *Saronic Gulf Islands and Kythira.*

Unfortunately, to travel from these to those of other groups will
inevitably involve considerable time spent on the journey whether
you choose to travel by air or sea.

For those interested in planning journeys to islands outside the
Ionian group, reliable information is difficult to come by even in
Greece. The weekly (daily in high season) print out from NTOG
offices covers sailings from all ports. *Greek Travel Pages* and *Key
Travel Guide* are books rather than papers or magazines which
include details of local and international sailings, rail and coach
services plus airline schedules; but neither is completely reliable and
the latter doesn't contain an index or list of contents, which makes
it difficult to use. The GTP can be obtained in Britain, tel. 081 876
2131. The paper *Journey to Greece* is no longer published.

FIVE

Accommodation

All the islands have a variety of accommodation available, to be found predominantly in the main town and to a lesser extent the other centres of population. Names of hotels with category, telephone number and location are listed in the individual island chapters.

What to expect

The local tourist police and NTOG allocate a category for all rooms to let both in private houses and hotels. This is decided by the standard and amount of facilities available. Something like a telephone in the room can upgrade it from a C to a B. The standard varies from one island to another and of the islands covered by this book, Paxos is by far the most expensive; but to put it in proportion, this means paying about an extra £6 per night there.

One characteristic of Greek rooms is that they are smaller than you may be used to and although the furniture is kept to a minimum it is often necessary to organise a one-way system around the room! Another is that the sheets seem to have been carefully measured to exactly fit the top of the bed with no allowance for tucking in at the bottom, top or sides! If you are used to more than one pillow, improvisation is called for.

Conventional baths are about as rare in Greece as Turks, and showers are the norm. Some islands experience a shortage of water in the summer and many water heating systems use solar panels, which means that your shower will be hotter at night than in the morning. Some have electrical back-up for the winter and the controls look like a fuse box with a round knob bearing "O" and "I" symbols. You may be allowed to turn on the water heater yourself but many Greeks seem to believe that these controls are beyond the understanding of most tourists! Towels and soap are provided but you may have to ask for them.

The room category and basic and extras charges are shown on an official card which must be displayed and is usually pinned behind the door, but in Paxos the room owners were unable to comply with this law as the police hadn't received the information required from NTOG. The prices shown are the maximum the owner is allowed to charge by law but if business is slack he may be willing to accept less. If the room charge does not include the price of showers, this will also be shown on the card, so look here for otherwise hidden extras. The various categories are: Luxury, A, B, C, D and E.

On most islands, people meet the ferries and cries of "Rooms, rooms" indicate their purpose. This practice is illegal but tolerated. The hotel and room representatives judge the new arrival by his/her appearance and approach those they think most suited to their accommodation. Many establishments run mini buses to transport you from the port to your room.

Camping

It is strictly illegal to sleep on beaches with or without camping equipment but, except for town beaches, the police turn a blind eye until prompted into action by local hotel and room owners. If all official accommodation becomes full (as it can) then sleeping under the stars is permitted as long as no fire of any kind is started either deliberately or accidentally. If you do start a fire, you are automatically provided with free accommodation for a minimum of two months in a Greek prison!

Camping grounds are a rarity and seldom meet the demand. The authorities are now providing financial aid to those who plan to build camp sites but as they require a large plot of land and must have a high standard of facilities, they are still a costly venture.

There is no camping allowed on Paxos and this is not likely to change as the islanders don't want this type of visitor, who often has little money to leave behind.

SIX

Food, drink and leisure activities

Food and where to eat

Most people will have eaten in a Greek restaurant in their home country at least once. If you have ever ordered *mezedes* you will have a good idea of the character of Greek food as it consists of a little of most of the dishes on the menu. Because most of the Greek restaurants in the UK are Cypriot owned, there will be slight variations in flavourings and of course the selection may be more limited by the difficulty in obtaining fresh ingredients, such as octopus and squid, which are readily available in Greece.

One major difference however will be the temperature of the food. In Greece it is unusual to find dishes served hotter than warm. This is not due to poor service or lack of facilities but is the way Greek people are used to serving and eating their food.

Centuries ago, each village had a central kitchen where the food was prepared for the entire community and a member of each family would take the appropriate containers to the kitchen and return with the family's share of the food at meal times. On the way home, the food would cool considerably and this is said to be the reason why they developed the habit of eating luke-warm meals.

Because not many Greek kitchens have an oven, just hot plates, you can often see the women taking containers of food ready for cooking to the bakers shop where, for a small fee, their cakes or joint of meat are cooked for them.

Breakfast The Greek people do not place much importance on breakfast and the NTOG is at present encouraging hotels to offer an alternative to the "continental breakfast" that consists of tea or coffee, toast, butter, jam and sometimes a piece of madeira cake.

Many cafés advertise "English breakfast"; however, if you choose sausages with your eggs, you will find them very "un-English" and more like little spicy frankfurters, tasty nevertheless. The ham is rather like salami but the bacon is what we are used to and of a high quality.

Most cafés use evaporated milk in coffee which is always called "Nescafé" to distinguish it from Greek coffee (it will be instant, though not necessarily that particular brand). Also, you can expect to have hot milk to go with your morning cup of tea! The butter is unsalted and the apricot marmalade bears a striking resemblance to apricot jam (delicious).

Tavernas
They vary in standard and prices but generally serve inexpensive traditional dishes which you select by going into the kitchen and pointing at what you want. This is an excellent way of ensuring that you like the look of what you order and of overcoming any language problems, although most owners and waiters speak at least enough English to cover all eventualities in their work. Only a very few *tavernas* serve desserts or coffee and you are expected to go elsewhere for "afters".

Restaurants
Their main difference from *tavernas* is that they are open at lunch time as well as in the evening and generally have a larger selection of food that may include steaks and some French and English dishes. They may also provide a small selection of desserts, coffee and after dinner drinks.

Zaharoplastéons
These cake shops sell gateaux, pastries and yoghourt to eat on the premises or take away. Coffee, tea, soft drinks, liqueurs and spirits are served but seldom wine or beer. It is to these shops you come for the sweet course of your meal and after dinner drinks. They generally keep shop hours.

Cafenións
All types of alcohol, soft and hot drinks are sold with a small selection of cakes and such foods that can be eaten with cocktail sticks (the law decrees) but this is often stretched to include fried eggs and omelettes, at which time a fork will be supplied.

Ouzerías
The Greek men (especially those whose working life is over) spend a large part of each day in a café or *ouzeria* watching the world go by or discussing politics, emphasising each point with energetic hand

Even though most houses in Corfu now have an adequate supply of clean water, Greek women of all ages still prefer to make the daily trip with various containers to the village spring as they believe that drinking water from this source has a better purity and taste.

gestures and raised voices. The latter is often confused by foreigners as a sign of a heated row in progress but this doesn't follow in Greece. A friendly but enthusiastic conversation can often include the participants yelling at each other!

On offer you will find Nescafé and Greek coffee, *ouzo, Metaxa* cognac, beer, soft drinks and a few pastries. If you order *ouzo* or cognac, be sure to order some *mezes* which complement the drinks. They are small plates of tomato, cucumber, bread with *tsatsiki, taramasalata* and anchovies and, of course, olives. At about a hundred drachmas, it is also excellent value.

If you are watching the sunset from one of these establishments, you will be able to enjoy some of the grilled octopus that is served at this time of day. The octopus have to be tenderised which explains why people can be seen apparently taking out a bad temper on the unresisting (lifeless) octopus. They are hung up to dry in the sun so watch your head as you walk under the awnings! Small pieces of the grilled tentacles are served on sticks with lemon juice and it

is customary to drink the remaining juice from the saucer, it is also
the best bit in my opinion! Don't be put off by its appearance, it
is delicious.

Menus

A popular source of tourist entertainment are the bilingual menus
found in all eating places. The variety of spelling mistakes can be
hilarious and it is occasionally impossible to work out what they are
trying to say. I can recommend "roast staff" from a *taverna* in
Syros where presumably one of the waiters fell foul of the chef. I
must thank Barbara Lightfoot of Stoke on Trent for informing me
of the delights of: "smal chops lamp", "braised red mallet", "veal
looked in pitcher" and "porgy"! (Perhaps you would like to send
me any howlers you find for inclusion in future editions).

Although the menus are lengthy, only the dishes with prices
beside them are available. The two prices for each dish are with and
without tax so the latter is purely academic. It is usual to leave a 10
per cent tip for the waiter and some small change for the boy who
laid the table and brought the drinks, although there is the same
ambiguity as at home about whether the service charge has already
been added. The boy however will get a very low wage and doesn't
receive a share of whatever you leave on the saucer. He is only
entitled to whatever is left directly on the table, usually near the edge
of a plate.

Meat When you look at the dishes on offer in the kitchen, the meat
will probably look as if it died of old age and has been dried out
even more in the cooking. Don't you believe it! If the cook can
manage to get it on to the plate before it disintegrates, you will see
how deceptive appearances can be.

Fish and shell fish In fish tavernas you choose your fish from a
refrigerated display cabinet and it is then cooked for you. Price is
by weight and is not as cheap as you might expect.

Live lobster seems to be the most common item on menus in
Paxos although the "creature" concerned is often more correctly
described as a crayfish. Fish are divided into classes and priced
accordingly but it is sometimes hard to agree with the categories and
some of the more lowly specimens can taste superior to the first class
types.

Drinks

Greek coffee This is similar to Turkish coffee but I don't suggest you order it as such. It comes with varying amounts of sugar and is always served black in a *demi-tasse* with a glass of cold water. Never stir it and beware of the considerable amount of sediment in the bottom. You drink it: without sugar — *skéto;* with a little sugar — *médrio;* incredibly sweet — *gleekó.*

Retsina Wine containers used to be made of hide treated with tree sap or resin. This flavoured the contents and the Greeks developed a taste for it this way and so today they add resin to some of the many local wines purely for the taste. This is definitely an acquired taste but at 300 drachmas a bottle, some feel the incentive to acquire it!

When drinking any alcoholic beverage in Greece, it is customary to chink glasses before drinking and with each refill. The origin of this custom is said to be that the Gods decreed that wine should please all five senses. The only one not obviously satisfied was hearing, hence chinking glasses.

Wine Those of you who enjoy being able to expound on which end of which vineyard the grapes came from for each glass of vintage French wine, may be a little disappointed in the Greek wines. Very few if any eating places in Corfu or Paxos stock imported wines although there can be a large selection of the local produce. My own preference is for the rosé wines but I have never been noted for having a refined palate.

An exclusive and elusive brew

Corfu boasts a wine that has sufficient quality to ensure that it is scarce. Only one off licence in San Rocco square stocks the produce of the famous Theotoki cellars. I couldn't afford it and so didn't taste it! Those of you with enough resources and inclination might be kind enough to let me know what it is like!

Beer In Greece beer always means lager although a "black lager" called Amstel Bok has lately come onto the market — and quickly been withdrawn again by subsequently furnitureless bar owners, as even the few customers that weren't seeking to become inebriated suddenly found themselves aggressively plastered on its barley wine type brew.

In addition to Amstel and what are described as the "green beers" (the label not the liquid) a variety of pretty little bottles of gold foiled German brews with unpronounceable names were imported in a ruse to be able to offer nothing else and therefore take a luxury price from those who just wanted a cheap half pint to sit in front of all evening.

Recent legislation has decontrolled the price of many items that were previously strictly regulated and beer is one of them. The price of a 750ml tin of the cheapest beer is now 170drs.

Ouzo An aniseed flavoured spirit made from the grape skins is clear until water is added at which time it turns milky white. It also has an uncanny knack of making you think that you are perfectly sober until you get up, at which time a battle ensues for control of your legs that you are unlikely to win with dignity!

Cognac Locally produced brandies are slightly sweeter than those produced in France but are enjoyable and, at 120drs a time, very inexpensive. Votry's does have a slight flavour of ouzo about it but the Metaxa goes down very nicely. Duty free bottled five star Greek brandy works out at just £5 for 750mls.

Raki Sometimes known as Souma this colourless spirit is very popular with the locals. The taste and more particularly the aroma varies greatly. There was one which had such a revolting smell that, try as I might, I couldn't get it near enough to taste it.

The Greeks never seem to suffer the day after a heavy drinking session and this is probably due to the fact that large glasses of cold water are served with all spirits and they never drink without taking a little food at the same time.

In recent years we have sadly seen the appearance of the "Bomba", which is the name given to an abominable system of raking a few extra drachmas profit from the tourists. These drinks have been diluted with methylated spirits and intoxicate much quicker than normal with the most awful suffering the next day. It isn't even safe to order a drink from an unopened bottle of a brand name spirit as many are bottled under licence in Greece and, although some of the illegal operators have been caught, it is likely that others haven't. This is the reason for even a small bar having two or three opened bottles of the same drink as they have to keep a supply of the real thing for the locals or those that order the spirit neat and without ice.

The practice is justified by the belief that most tourists just want to get drunk as quickly and as cheaply as possible, and we don't generally do much to convince them otherwise.

Entertainment

The variety of nightlife on the islands is of course proportional to the extent of its involvement in the tourist industry.

Discotheques

These places vary greatly from an improvised dance floor in the middle of a field to fairly sophisticated night spots. The disc jockeys seemed to be picked for fairness of face rather than musical knowledge or technique and generally have a complete disregard for whether anyone else is enjoying the music. Not all discotheques have an admission charge but where they do it will include the price of your first drink. The cheapest way to get round the higher drink prices is to buy a bottle of wine and share it but they are catching on to that and often don't serve wine or beer.

Bars

The dividing line between a bar and a disco is fine to the casual observer but in legal terms is strictly defined. How rigidly the regulations are adhered to depends on how often the police pass by but some bar owners who have got fed up with appearing on thirty-one separate charges each month in court and dutifully paying the fines have obtained a disco licence and now wider and more substantial bar tops are being installed to cope with the recent trend of dancing on and not in the bar.

Bouzoukis

There is never an admission charge as such but on weekends and bank holidays a reservation fee is needed for tables, and the length of time they are required affects the price. The usual drink is whisky, which may be placed on the empty tables and be priced at anything between 15,000 and 40,000drs a bottle! Other drinks are similarly priced and the large selection of food is very expensive.

Live Greek music is played incredibly loudly by a group of at least six musicians, one or more of whom will sing. The locals tend to get enthusiastic on an evening at the bouzouki and plates are broken and tables overturned as gestures of appreciation of the entertainment. Waiters immediately rush up and replace what ever has been broken whilst keeping a careful tally. Perhaps the knowledge that to take the family there costs a month's wages helps promote enjoyment.

Greek dancing

I don't think it is possible not to enjoy watching the local men dancing, at least on the first occasion. Whether it is a single old timer dancing because he just can't help himself or a group of young lads out to impress the girls, you can't help being caught up in the atmosphere it creates and the skill involved. By all means clap along to the music but lone females should realise the significance of crouching at the edge of the dance floor and clapping on their own to a male dancing, as in some places it implies a very intimate relationship. You might prefer to watch the dancing in a bar or disco rather than a bouzouki where it tends to get too crowded to be able to see what is happening. Many bars have someone used to teaching tourists the steps and they have a strange knack of conveying what you are supposed to do next even if not in words.

Cinemas

Many islands have open air cinemas that add an extra dimension to watching old movies. Most films shown in the summer are in English with Greek subtitles. Comedies are less suitable than thrillers or westerns as the locals often read the subtitles and start laughing, preventing you from hearing the punch line in the dialogue.

The indoor cinemas are all no smoking areas and a lounge will be provided for smoking. It is customary to tip the usherette between 20 and 50drs for having shown you to your numbered seat. For some obscure reason these buildings are usually freezing cold all year round in contrast to the open air cinemas with the warm evening breezes and clouds of mosquitos.

Sailing

Both islands have sailing boats for hire and it may be possible to make arrangements to hire privately owned vessels from locals or resident expatriates.

Flotilla holidays There are a small number of mainland companies which organise flotilla holidays. The selection of islands to be visited is often decided by the consensus of opinion among the passengers; and so you may see a large number of sailing boats moored in the harbour. Be warned that they can be moored there for six months or more as, in the past, the island port police have declared the boats to carry inadequate safety equipment and have impounded them for eventual auction to cover the mooring fees and fines. This of course left the unfortunate holidaymakers stranded, so check out the company first if you plan to use this method of getting about.

Some of the package holiday companies, especially the local firms have arrangements for booking craft at the same time as your holiday. See Chapter 3 for details.

Swimming

One of the joys of the beaches is that swimming is safe for both adults and children, as undercurrents and undersea shelves are very rare indeed. Swimming is an enjoyable part of most people's holiday both because of the need to cool off intermittently when sunbathing and because the Ionian Sea has an enticing variety of all the shades of blue and green imaginable, that proves irresistible to young and old alike. Many beaches are bordered by rocky outcrops where snorkellers can explore the variety of marine life found there.

In the shallows, if you stay still long enough, tiny transparent fish, with markings on the tail that look like eyes at the other end, will gently nibble at your legs possibly to remove the grains of salt that the evaporating seawater leaves.

Beaches

Most Greek beaches are thoroughly cleared of seaweed and litter at the start of the season. One of the reasons why sleeping on the beaches is opposed is because of the human waste and rubbish that has been left there to spoil the enjoyment of others in the past. Enough said. Both islands have beaches where you find sunbeds, umbrellas, windsurfers, skiing equipment and canoes.

Nudism

The Greek people do not understand the joys of swimming and sunbathing naked or even topless. On my home island, the locals have been prompted into printing notices reminding people that it is illegal and suggesting where they should go to prevent causing offence. Where idiotic individuals have been callous enough to peel off on town beaches, you will find mothers feel obliged to take an alternative route home with school children.

Corfu has one beach suitable for nudism and discretion can be used in other areas away from the crowds and in particular Greek families, some of whom still believe that you can catch AIDS from bathing in the water near someone naked. Many holidays have been spoilt when offenders were taken to court, fined and had their passports endorsed to prevent subsequent re-entry to the country. The police have been known to don swimming trunks and to look for naturists before returning in uniform to make the arrests.

Diving

A new law has been introduced that forbids the use of air tanks for diving unless a permit is held by the diver. This is to prevent the removal of antiquities and damage to unexcavated archaeological sites on the sea bottom. The companies that organise diving expeditions have such permits and will help you make the necessary arrangements for participation.

SEVEN

Shopping

There are few things that cost significantly more in Greece to make it worth bringing them from home. Photographic film is marginally cheaper at home and black and white film is almost impossible to find in Greece. If you plan to be self-catering, beef stock cubes, coffee whitener and bran are about the only things not available at the supermarkets. Double the cost in Greece are paperback books, and I consequently enter a plea on behalf of Greek island resident expatriates who would dearly love to get their hands on some fresh reading material: don't throw books and newspapers away, try and find someone to give them to or persuade your hotel to start a small library. Many of the travel agencies have a small selection of used books that can be taken in exchange for leaving a similar volume.

Shop opening hours

Like all the times quoted in this chapter, these must be taken as a guide only, but in general they are 08.00 to 13.00 hours and 17.00 to 20.00 hours Monday to Saturday, with no evening opening on Mondays and Wednesdays. There have been many strikes lately by shop employees protesting at the opening hours. When they eventually won their case there were further strikes to have the hours changed back again. The winter opening hours currently in use are Mondays 13.00 to 19.00 hours, Tuesdays to Saturdays 09.00 to 19.00 hours, closed all day on Sundays. Souvenir shops and boutiques may not bother to close in the afternoon and may be open on Sundays and late into the evening depending on the number of potential buyers on the streets. Most shops close for the various religious holidays and, in addition to these, shops have their own name days according to the type of shop. No warning is posted, even in Greek, of these holidays to enable you to stock up on food, or other things you might need.

What to buy

Everyone has different ideas about which souvenirs are tasteful or gaudy but Greece has a large selection of the former. Practical cheesecloth dresses, attractive ceramics, handmade jewellery, fringed scarves, dazzling posters and postcards, leather shoes, brassware and statuettes are just some of the souvenirs that are worth buying for reasons other than purely as a holiday memento. Particular bargains are: Greek cigarettes, cognac, wines, suntan oil, cheesecloth dresses and silver jewellery. (See appendix C for table of size comparisons.)

Weight
Almost everything in Greece is sold by weight in kilos, including string, wine, paper and nails: 1 kilo = 2.2 lb.

Books and newspapers

Both islands covered in this book stock English newspapers which are priced according to their weight and the published price of the paper: 350 to 600drs. Some glossy magazines are available but you can expect to pay as much as you would for a fairly thick novel at home.

Kiosks

Found on most street corners these orangy brown painted constructions are known as *peripteros* in Greek. Somehow they manage to stock a larger selection of goods than most Woolworths, including cigarettes, matches, sweets, nuts, chocolate, razors, pens, contraceptives, aspirins, vapour rub, throat sweets, newspapers, books, magazines, maps, adhesive tape, paper, envelopes and a multitude of other things. Most have a metered telephone for public use.

The occupants are often disabled or war veterans as kiosks are State allocated. Opening hours vary but many only close from midnight to 07.00 hours.

Banks and currency

Banks

Both Corfu and Paxos have banks but at the latter money can only be withdrawn from accounts based in Paxos or Kerkyra. Corfu has a branch of Barclay's Bank in San Rocco Square (see Chapter 14). Both islands have post offices.

If you plan to stay in Greece longer than three months, save the pink exchange slips as you will need them when applying for a visa renewal.

Opening hours are from 08.00 to 14.00 hours (13.30 Friday) Monday to Friday. Where a large number of tourists are found, the banks may stay open later and may even open on Saturdays for exchange only. These hours will be displayed outside the bank. Some Greek banks have been on strike on and off for the last three years but an exchange desk sometimes remains open.

Currency

The exchange rate for sterling varies from day to day. Currently (January 1991) £1 = 300 drachmas. The amount of drachmas you can buy in your home country and re-exchange after the holiday is regulated by Greek law. Any British bank will be able to provide up-to-date details before your departure and also order the appropriate amount of drachmas if you wish to have some cash ready for your arrival in Greece.

There are also regulations that demand that large amounts of imported foreign currency be declared at your port of arrival. The current amount is always displayed inside the airport, passenger transfer buses and other conspicuous places near immigration desks but it is usually higher than the amount the average holidaymaker would bring so doesn't normally create a problem. If you are bringing a substantial amount of sterling into Greece then it is definitely wiser to join the endless queue to the tiny office that provides absolutely no privacy in which to display your wealth to the customs official. If for any reason you still have over the legal limit when leaving Greece and are unlucky enough to have it found on your person at the port of departure, it may be impounded.

Bank Notes These come in increasing size according to value, and in various colours. Denominations are: 50 drachmas (light blue), now no longer officially legal tender but seldom refused (the National Bank will exchange any you get stuck with); 100 drachmas (pinky red); 500 drachmas (green); 1,000 drachmas (brown); and 5,000 drachmas (navy).

An indication of the oppressively high inflation is that, while a year or so ago shopkeepers became angry when given 5,000 drachma notes, these now present no problem; a 10,000 drachma note will soon be in circulation.

Coins The coins are currently being changed and this has led to a needless muddle as there are now great similarities in the size and colour of new one and two drachma coins and old two and twenty drachma coins. In the case of the latter problem, at least for a while, the new small twenty drachma coins are likely to be shinier than the old style two drachma coins. To summarise the coins in circulation: ½p-size bronze 1 drachma, ½p-size bronze 2 drachmas, 20p-size two drachmas, 20p-size silver five drachmas, 2p-size silver ten drachmas, 10p-size silver twenty drachmas, and 20p-size brass fifty drachmas.

Supermarket prices may have two figures after a decimal point. This is because the drachma is theoretically divided into a hundred lepta. No lepta coins exist and this is just a way of inching up prices.

Opposite: *Corfu's most photographed spot where the islets of Vlacherna and Pontikonissi (Mouse Island) have become the symbol of the island.*

Overleaf: *The tempting and colourful displays outside the greengrocer's shop are somehow much more spectacular than at home.*

Post offices

Post offices *(Taheedroméeo)* are easily distinguished by their bright yellow sign posts with black lettering. The same colour scheme is found on the post boxes. Opening hours are from 07.30 to 14.15 hours, larger branches may stay open for an additional half hour; closed Saturdays and Sundays. All post offices on the smaller islands and the main post office on the larger islands provide a Poste Restante service. Passports must be presented when collecting letters and parcels. There may be some confusion over which letter of the Greek alphabet your post has been filed under, so ask anyone writing to you to use only your Christian and surname and to underline the surname. This avoids the possibility of it being filed under Mr or Mrs.

Postage stamps can be bought at shops selling postcards. They are allowed to charge 10 per cent above the face value of the stamps.

Post offices now also undertake all foreign exchange transactions, which is very useful on smaller islands that don't have banks. In peak season the smaller offices may run out of drachmas as the float is insufficient to cope with large numbers of people wishing to exchange cheques or cash drachmas.

Opening a post office account in Athens is an ideal way of avoiding having to transport all your cash from island to island. Passports are always needed when making withdrawals.

Telephone offices

The abbreviation for the Greek name for these offices is OTE. pronounced owtay. Every island has at least one but they vary from large buildings to someone's spare room! International calls and local calls can be made from here but local calls are not allowed from the OTEs in Athens, you must use a kiosk.

The 'phone booth contains a meter and a table to tell you the cost of various meter readings, e.g. 100 units = 1,000 drachmas. The length of time for each unit depends, of course, on where you are calling. Before dialling, the meter must be at zero. The assortment of noises made by the telephone system is very different from ours. The ringing tone at first sounds like our engaged tone but the notes are coupled and have a long pause between couples.

When your call is completed, you pay at the desk having indicated which booth you have used. A receipt will be given.

Opening hours 08.00 to 14.30 hours and 17.30 to 21.00 hours Monday to Friday, half day only Saturday; but these hours vary enormously from island to island.

Transfer charge and person to person calls will be placed for you but it may entail waiting in the office for up to two hours. These offices also handle **telegrams** but it is always cheaper to telephone.

Telephone kiosks

Kiosks with blue or orange bands at the top of the sides. The blue ones use ten drachma coins which must be inserted before dialling but after lifting the receiver. The orange booths can take international calls and use ten, twenty and 50 drachma coins. A tiny dim red light goes on a split second before you get cut off and there are no pips to tell you to put in more money. Unused coins should be returned to you when you replace the receiver but this system is as prone to faults as our own. None of the kiosks takes incoming calls. Very little vandalism of 'phone boxes is found in Greece.

The kiosks known as *peripteros* have metered 'phones from where you can make local or international calls but enquire about the cost of a ten-unit call before you begin, as some owners illegally charge much more per unit than the official rate. A local call that uses one unit is always slightly more expensive than a tenth of a ten-unit call charge.

EIGHT

Your health and comfort

General health

It is not necessary to have any inoculations before visiting Greece unless you have recently visited an area where yellow fever or cholera are endemic.

The main health problem you may encounter is from the laxative properties of the olive oil, which forms an ingredient for almost everything except bread! A change of diet has the same effect, so don't rush to the chemist for antibiotics at the first sign of gastric disturbances. A kaolin mixture or Lomotil taken after each bowel movement gives speedy relief and can be purchased from local chemists without prescription. Remember to maintain an adequate fluid and salt intake or you could get some painful stomach cramps.

Medical care

All islands have at least one doctor. On smaller islands, the doctor is probably newly trained and doing a form of community work in lieu of his National Service. The Useful Information sections under the Corfu and Paxos chapters explain how to contact the nearest hospital and doctor. In some places the surgeries double as the only pharmacy. Opening hours are posted outside. In case of serious illness, patients are transported by boat or helicopter to the nearest hospital.

Theoretically if you obtain form E.111 from an office of the Department of Health and Social Security (see leaflet S.A.30) before leaving the UK, you will be entitled to treatment at a token cost. In practice, the problems of getting the necessary forms completed by the doctor make this a nonsense. A consultation will cost approximately 3,000 drachmas.

Medical insurance

Medical insurance to cover accidents and emergency treatments is recommended for travellers to Greece. Remember that there are few hospitals in the islands and should you need hospital treatment the costs of being transported there — even apart from the treatment itself — could be very high indeed. Your travel agent will give you the latest information about insurance policies. Check that the sum you are insured for is adequate. Emergency surgery such as an appendectomy, for example, can be very costly. If you were unfortunate to need anything like this, it would also delay your return home — so make sure that the medical insurance you take out is realistic.

Hazards

Greece is the home of a few nasties including small white scorpions, black widow and brown hermit spiders plus two species of poisonous snakes. You are extremely unlikely to encounter any of these little treasures whose venom is rarely fatal. Should you be unlucky enough to be bitten or stung, don't try to imitate anything you may have seen in the movies as this only speeds up the spread of the venom. Get help as quickly as possible giving a description of what "got you".

There are few strong currents or undercurrents on the island beaches and the only hazards are sea urchins and jellyfish, both of which are painful. Leave sea urchin spines alone, trying to get them out only pushes them further in. Apply some olive oil and keep pressure off the affected area, they will work their own way out. Jellyfish can sting even when dead and beached, so if you find one why not move it out of harm's way with a stick, as other people may not be as observant as you.

Sunburn

There is one very serious danger lurking for the unprotected: the sun. The gentle breeze is very pleasant but it masks the strength of the sun. This is particularly true on the sundecks of the ferries, where you can relax comfortably for long enough to start your holiday with third degree burns. Sun screens and after-sun creams are available more cheaply than at home and with a mind-boggling selection. Take sunbathing slowly at first. Whatever you do, never fall asleep in the sun.

Toilets

Greek toilets are not the sort of places in which you would want to spend any length of time. Most are of the type we are used to but some are the "squatting" variety. In the latter be careful of losing the contents of your pockets. In all toilets, a basket or bin is provided into which you must put all used toilet paper as the plumbing can't cope with it. To operate the flush, push the plunger underneath the cistern.

Men's and women's toilets are differentiated by the usual trousered and skirted figures on the doors. A single toilet usually bears the letters "WC".

Public toilets are rare but all eating places have to have them by law. Only a few will insist that they are for the use of customers only. The Greek word for toilet is pronounced *too allétta.*

Drinking water

The water is safe to drink in all parts of Greece but the taste varies. On Paxos it is very briny and fresh water is sold by street vendors. Bottled water is available at all supermarkets for about 150 drachmas for 1½ litres. These plastic bottles are useful for taking to the beach (and light to bring back to town for disposal!).

The water generally has a high concentration of minerals and a photographer friend tells me that he finds it impossible to get any of his developing chemicals to dissolve in it.

NINE

Getting about

Time and distance

Greek time is one or two hours ahead of that in England depending on the time of year: the adjustments to and from daylight saving time are out of synchronisation with the rest of Europe. This is not the only difference, as the whole concept of time bears no similarity to our own. Expressions such as morning, midday, afternoon and evening are so flexible as to be meaningless. If you are trying to make an appointment of any kind, specify the exact hour and even then, unless you say "English time", rendezvous will be anything up to two hours later or "Greek time".

Distance is equally flexible and "near", "just around the corner" and "a few minutes walk" can turn out to be a few kilometres.

Public transport

Taxis

In the centre of Athens it is very difficult to get a taxi even though these bright yellow cars account for about 50 per cent of the traffic. The problem is caused by the regulations introduced to lessen smog in the city, which stipulate that vehicles may only be used on alternate days according to the registration numbers. Consequently car owners must find an alternative method of getting to work — and they appropriate the taxis.

Taxi ranks at Syntagma Square, underground stations and both airports are some good places to try. Otherwise you have to stand somewhere where the occupied taxis are forced to slow down or stop, traffic lights for example, and shout your destination through the window. Each passenger will pay the full fare unless you are travelling together therefore picking up single passengers rather than a couple is more lucrative.

While on most islands the taxis are metallic grey, there are variations.

Buses

On the small islands, buses have a relaxed atmosphere and it doesn't matter which door you use to get in. On the mainland the pace of life is that much faster and you have to get in at the front and pay the exact fare into a box near the driver. If you don't know the fare, have plenty of change handy. Keep the ticket as many routes are checked on every journey by an inspector.

There is little uniformity in the appearance of bus stop signs but they ususaly have " ΣΤΑΣΙΣ " on them or the picture of a bus.

Trains

Operating only in Athens and its suburbs is a single route electric train. These trains mostly run above ground from Kifissia to Piraeus and are useful for getting from Athens to Piraeus. The fare is 40 drachmas. Ticket offices don't open until about 08.00 and so if the man in the office is ignoring you, just walk through the turnstile and tickets will not be checked at the other end. Later in the day you must buy a valid ticket from either the machines or office and retain it for inspection at the other end.

Walking

Crossing the road in Athens takes either nerves of steel or suicidal tendencies. They have plenty of red and green men to advise you but the trouble is that when the green man is lit, it only means that traffic wishing to go straight ahead is being shown a red light. Where drivers can turn right they may still have a green light and so you have to dodge them.

There seems to be no penalty for stopping on the zebra crossing while waiting for the lights to change and you often have to pick your way around and squeeze between vehicles on the striped area.

Motorbike and moped rental

The majority of the bikes have seen better days and survived some rough treatment that the mechanics have a knack of camouflaging with a coat of paint. Some important points to remember when hiring a vehicle:

● Make sure it works! Take it for a test drive which will also —

● Ensure that you can handle it.

● Negotiate the price, especially if hiring for more than one day. Does the price include petrol?

● Get the 'phone number of the agency in case of breakdown. All of them have their own breakdown trucks and they don't sit idle for long.

● Seriously consider asking for one of their crash helmets. At no extra charge, these look like multi-coloured tortoises and while they won't do a thing to improve your image they may prove to be your salvation: there are so many "holidaydrivers" around in the summer that even if *you* know what you are doing, you may fall foul of someone else who doesn't. Accidents are literally an everyday occurrence. Most people get away with cuts and bruises but every time you see that helicopter overhead, someone has been badly injured and is on his way to the hospital.

● Make a firm arrangement about returning the bike. The expression used may be "for the day" but if you return a bike after 19.00 hours, you will find yourself unpopular with the employee who has had to work late for you. If you want to keep it until the next morning, make it clear.

● Be sure you take notice of the traffic signs (the same as in Europe). Many of the roads are closed to motorbikes and mopeds even though cars are permitted. Keep your eyes open and don't forget that they drive on the right hand side in Greece!

● Where island roads are of a poor standard, choose a bike with large wheels.

● Resist the temptation to take corners at speed.

If your bike does break down and your knowledge of their mechanical workings is limited or non-existent, try taking the petrol cap off and then rocking the bike from side to side to hear if you have got any petrol left (petrol = *vin zeé nee)*. Have a look for the sparkplug which is usually found between the front wheel (that round thing) and a grooved thing the size of a small loaf of bread that burns your fingers when you touch it. If you locate the sparkplug make sure that there is a cap sitting firmly on top of it rather than waving about in the air on the end of its cable. If you can't find the sparkplug, see if you can spot a hole where one used to be, and then walk back and look for it.

Remember it is illegal to drive motorised bikes through towns between the hours of 13.00 and 17.00 or indeed to make any loud noise.

Car hire

Corfu has a bewildering number of car rental agencies, but on Paxos it is necessary to book in advance of the day that you require a vehicle so that it can be sent over on the ferries from either Corfu or the mainland.

TEN

Customs and things you should know

Worry beads

Most Greek men have at least one set of worry beads which they produce at moments of tension, boredom or relaxation. These can be made of metal, plastic or wood and do not, as might be suspected derive from the rosary (in fact some scholars say that the rosary derives from them . . .) Some men are very adept at making the beads fly up and down their fingers and techniques vary. You will not see women using worry beads.

Drinking

As mentioned in Chapter Six, each refilled glass should be chinked with those of your companions. There are a variety of salutations used and as these can be rather confusing, just repeat whatever your host says. Be very careful when chinking not to knock the top of his glass with the bottom of your glass as this amounts to wishing a curse on him; and should you inadvertently bring the base of your glass down vertically on the top of his, you have wished a curse on him and his family. The best thing to do in this instance would be to quickly snatch the glass from his hand and spill the contents on the floor, but you won't be too popular in a carpeted restaurant!

Gestures — and avoiding trouble

One gesture that can be very confusing is the one used to indicate a negative reply to a question. The head is tipped sharply back and may be accompanied by a clicking noise made with the tongue. This gesture can be modified until only an eyebrow is moved almost imperceptibly and it takes a while to get used to it — you tend to think that either they haven't heard the question at all or are asking you to repeat or explain it.

The Greeks have a hand gesture that is far worse than our reversed victory sign in its meaning. To hold up your hand at eye level with fingers spread and palm outwards at someone is the worst possible insult and virtually a challenge to a duel. Even worse is to use two hands! I couldn't understand the look of horror on someone's face when I tried to use sign language to convey that I would be back in ten minutes by pointing to my watch and then holding up the appropriate number of fingers!

The word *malláka* is used frequently in conversation by Greek males and is the derogatory name for someone who satisfies their own physical desires. This is always used light-heartedly (there are far worse for when they are serious) but it is never acceptable for foreigners to use this word no matter how close you are or how long you have known somebody.

The evil eye

The Greek people believe strongly in the power of the evil eye — which is thought to be put on anyone who causes another to be envious of them. The way to avoid it is to wear one of the blue eye beads you will see in souvenir shops; or, if you think you might be about to put it on someone, spit or make a noise similar to that of spitting. Should you wish to compliment someone on their baby, then you may be warned "Na mee ton (or 'tis')matee ah zees" and should then spit to avoid drawing the attention of ill luck.

The test to see if you have caused someone such envy as to have become "Matee asmenee" is to try to recite at speed a piece of religious text, such as The Lord's Prayer. If you can't complete it or get muddled then you have got the evil eye and must go to one of the ladies who sit outside larger churches and she will remove it for you.

Religion

The Greek Orthodox faith is predominant everywhere in Greece although some islands have a proportion of Catholics. Orthodoxism is a splinter of the Catholic religion and has no connection with the Pope.

The interior of this little church is typical of those found in all the villages, including some very isolated spots. Unfortunately these churches are more often than not locked, owing to some icons having been stolen in the past.

Services have a very relaxed atmosphere and no hymns or prayers are sung by the congregation. The faith seems to be strong and not as restrictive as some other forms of Christianity. Priests up to a certain "rank" are allowed to be married.

Churches and name days

The islands have literally hundreds of churches ranging from the very grand to those no bigger than the average garden shed! Every family tries to build a church at some time. Each church is named after a saint and in the smaller ones services are held only on the corresponding saint's day, once a year.

In the monasteries and larger churches, the whole village will attend services giving a festival atmosphere. Similarly all Greek people are named after saints and while birthdays are not celebrated, name days are marked by visiting with gifts the homes of fellow celebrants. There is little variety of names and so on the designated day for the most common names, such as Yannis and Kostas, restaurants and nightspots are well attended to the point of bursting!

Easter

Easter is a good time to visit Greece, especially Corfu, where the celebrations are known throughout the country to be at their most extravagant. Not seen in many other places is the custom of throwing unwanted plates and other ceramics onto the streets, which is said to represent the stoning of Judas, of whom in years gone by the unfortunate Jewish population of the city were unwilling symbols.

Bearing in mind that the Orthodox festival may be as much as a month later than the British Easter, these celebrations are as as enthusiastic as Christmas is in England (Christmas is a lesser festival in Greece). Good Friday is a day of mourning. On the Saturday everyone goes to church for a midnight service after which there may be a firework display and each household lights a candle and tries to carry it home still lit. If successful, this is a sign of good luck for the next year.

On Easter Sunday, the traditional meal is of roast lamb, and wine is free in restaurants and *tavernas* if you can find one open. People carry red eggs and the usual "good morning" or "good evening" is replaced by "Christ is risen" to which the reply is "truly risen".

Transport to and within Greece is generally full at this time, so if you are planning an Easter trip book well in advance.

ELEVEN

Introducing Corfu

Population: 97,000   *Highest point: 820m*
Area: 592 sq. km.   *Hotel beds: 25,667*

Corfu is the northernmost of the seven islands and half of its length
lies opposite the Albanian rather than the Greek mainland; so Corfu
is very much a border island both with Albania and the many ships
that plough the Italy/Yugoslavia to Patras route.

A large, densely populated and prosperous island, it has for
centuries held an appeal for those who travel. For the early
eccentrics and aristocrats whose characters and position respectively
enabled them to seek out such places, Corfu was somewhere that
they took to their hearts and left only reluctantly.

If for you the name Corfu has associations' only with those late-
saver advertisements in the travel agents' windows and holiday press
or is just another name on the airport departure board, it would be
easy to dismiss it as an island that has totally sold its soul to the
invading hordes of tourists. Statistics do little to dispel that image:
half a million visitors per year, two thirds of which are British, make
it the most popular Greek island, and it receives a quarter of all our
package holidaymakers. The image is true enough in places but the
resorts are self contained and outside of these areas there are still
smaller centres with a few hotels and places where you can get away
from it all. Corfu has something for everyone and plenty for those
interested in seeing all it has to offer.

The capital

The island is one of the few that visitors know by a different name
from that used by the local people and timetables will show details
of "Kerkyra" not Corfu. Not unusually for Greece, this is also the
name of the capital. Although the English road signs give distances

View over the Sinarades rooftops; the aged ceramic tiles are very photogenic.

to "Corfou", the city will be referred to in this book as Kerkyra to distinguish it from Corfu the island.

The capital is ideally placed approximately equidistant from the island's north and south points for an exploratory base, whether you travel by rented vehicle, public transport, on foot or a combination of these. There are only a few beaches in the immediate vicinity of the city and a limited number of hotels but the variety of traditional restaurants and the convenience of access to all the routes make up for this.

The airport

Corfu's airport on the outskirts of Kerkyra dates back to the Second World War when it was just a makeshift runway and a hut in the middle of a swamp! The facilities are more sophisticated today but the increase in the amount of traffic coming into the island means that there are occasions when the terminal buildings become sardine-tin-like. Construction is underway of a second terminal but it won't be completed until 1994 at the most optimistic estimate.

From left to right as you enter the building are: international arrivals, international departures, domestic departures and domestic arrivals. There are a bank, post office, a souvenir shop and a small duty free shop within the terminal. A tiny snack bar lurks beyond domestic departure Gate 6. A large display board gives details of the courtesy telephone service to hotels, apartment agencies, car rental companies and taxi firms.

Up to fifty five flights per day, mostly of charter aircraft, connect with all the British airports, Amsterdam, Dusseldorf, Frankfurt, Geneva, Milan, Rome and Stuttgart. The runway isn't long enough to cope with Jumbo aircraft but the 727s and 737s are accommodated.

Most flight arrivals are at night and, as the bank is closed outside of normal banking hours, it is fortunate for those passengers who have not brought drachmas with them that the taxi drivers are prepared to accept payment in most currencies, at a lower rate of exchange. Except for package holidaymakers and those that have availed themselves of the courtesy telephone system in the terminal building, the only way to get from the airport to the town is by taxi and the rank is conveniently outside the exit doors.

The ports

Corfu's two ports are within a short distance of each other in Kerkyra. International arrivals are to the new port, the most westerly of the two and in the suburb of Mandouki. When you descend from the ferry by vehicle, it isn't immediately obvious where you should go. The general direction to follow is left and on into the far right hand lane of the roads leading into the buildings where the customs officials will eventually arrive to inspect the vehicles.

Foot passengers proceed past the sniffer dogs into the left hand door of the same building. If you are arriving from another Greek port, you must say so should they invite you into "that little room". Outside are the usual selection of people looking for customers for hotels and camping grounds, and a taxi rank, but no bus service to take you the short distance into town.

The port building has a municipal information office which maintains that it is open to coincide with arrivals, a snack bar, exchange desk and desks of all the major shipping lines — these often turn out to be manned by a school boy who eventually arrives to open the gates to let passengers embark ten minutes after the ship was due to depart.

Corfu is linked to the following shipping routes:

- Corfu, Igoumenitsa, Patras.
- Corfu, Ancona.
- Corfu, Bari.
- Corfu, Brindisi.
- Corfu, Dubrovnik, Ancona.
- Corfu, Dubrovnik, Split, Rijeka.
- Corfu, Igoumenitsa, Paxos, Ithaki, Kefallonia, Patras.

Tickets for these services can be purchased from the appropriate office opposite the new port but not from the old port.

From the old port there are hourly departures to Igoumenitsa and the Paxos boats. Tickets are sold in the offices to the east of the port area (right as you face the sea) and information might be given from the port police hut in front of the square. There is a café to sit at if you have to wait.

TWELVE

Getting around Corfu

The roads

Corfu has thoroughfares of all sizes and standards, ranging from the footpath of deep sand to a newly asphalted dual carriageway first constructed by British troops during occupation of the islands.

Traffic in the capital

From both of the two ports the roads are fortunately two way systems, which gives you a chance to get orientated before proceeding into the town where two way traffic is the exception rather than the rule. Arseniou, the road on the hill to the east of the old port, has "Stop" signs which at first appear to be over cautious until you actually get round the corner and can appreciate the need for them — because the tour buses have to enter the opposite lane in order to negotiate the turn.

Getting around the capital inevitably takes you at some time to San Rocco Square where, even during the quieter hours, the traffic has serious problems which were apparently worsened by the system of traffic lights that have now been turned off. The congestion is caused by no one really knowing who has right of way and all being determined that it should be themselves!

To get from the west of San Rocco Square, also known as Platea Theotoki, into Alexandras where the post office is located, you must cross the two way flow of traffic in G. Theotoki Street. This is no easy feat, especially when everyone else behind you is honking impatiently for their turn at running the gauntlet. The best way of getting to the main OTE is outlined in Chapter 14.

Another hazardous spot in Kerkyra is at the start of Dimokrateous, as cars coming from Akademias aren't sufficiently warned that they are about to cross a two-way system and the result is sometimes "dodgems".

Polikroni Konstanta has been dug up in so many places that you bounce rather than drive along it!

In August the road by the old port often becomes completely jammed with Italian visitors and their vehicles and in 1989 a team of Italian traffic policemen were sent over to help cope with the congestion! Parking is nearly impossible even in the low season.

Going up to Kanoni, the route becomes one way just past the Analipsis signpost, and you have to continue up to the top and down again some 4km should you wish to change direction.

Out of town

There are a bewildering number of routes leaving Kerkyra for the various destinations. See the map of Kerkyra for details.

Coming from Sidari to Kerkyra at the point where the sign reads "Corfou 19Km", there is a junction that suddenly appears out of nowhere and if you are going at more than 30km/h you are already on the main route from Paleokastritsa before you have time to stop. Two kilometres further on towards Sidari you may come across a most peculiar hazard: the road covered with spiders the size of a 50p piece which hop about all over the place when you approach! Motor bike drivers whose passengers are of a squeamish disposition be warned. I encountered this phenomenon every day for a fortnight so it doesn't seem to be a rare occurrence.

The track from Aghios Mattheos to Paramona is awful and should be avoided by cars and all but Enduro bikes.

On the edge of Perivoli and in front of the bell tower is a nasty bend on this busy route and caution is needed.

At Perama there were deep channels across the road as a result of road works, often just around a blind bend; but they may well have completed the work there by the time you read this. There were extensive road works going on at Moraitika which similarly may have been completed.

Buses

To confuse the issue, there are two bus companies with separate depots in Kerkyra and in some villages these have separate stops. This means that if you happen to be waiting at the wrong one the driver is not allowed to stop and pick you up, as it amounts to piracy!

From two covered shelters in San Rocco Square the navy blue buses leave. The current timetable is displayed but, as the company office is at a vantage point elsewhere on the square, at times when there are enough people waiting, extra buses will be dispatched to cope with the demand. Similarly on rainy days schedules are changed from services taking people to beach resorts to services bringing people into Kerkyra for shopping and sightseeing. The routes are:

— Kerkyra to Dassia From 07.00 to 22.00, ½-hourly, 70drs.

— Kerkyra to Benitses From 07.00 to 21.30, hourly, 70drs.

— Kerkyra to Kanoni From 07.00 to 22.00, ½-hourly, 50drs.

— Kerkyra to Pelekas 07.00, 10.00, 12.00, 14.00, 16.00, 17.00 and 21.00 hrs, 70drs.

There are greatly reduced services on Sundays and holidays. No return tickets.

The light blue or greenish and cream buses of the KTEL national bus company leave from the terminus at the base of the New Fort and by the side of the large Agricultural Bank in Kerkyra. Tickets can be purchased from the ticket office or on the buses and the former system ensures you a seat. The routes are:

— Kerkyra to Paleokastritsa From 08.30 to 19.00, hourly or every 90 minutes, 200drs.

— Kerkyra to Glyfada From 06.45 to 17.30, approx every 90 minutes, 150drs.

— Kerkyra to Kassiopi From 05.45 to 16.00, sporadic 7 per day, 290drs.

— Kerkyra to Ipsos Pirgos From 07.15 to 19.30, sporadic 10 per day, 130 drs.

— Kerkyra to Sidari From 05.45 to 19.30, sporadic 7 per day, 280drs.

— Kerkyra to Aghios Stefanos (west) 06.00, 1300 and 15.30hrs, 360drs.

— Kerkyra to Roda and Anaharavi 05.45, 09.30, 13.30 and 16.00hrs, 320drs.

— Kerkyra to Kavos From 05.00 to 19.30, sporadic 11 per day, 370drs.

— Kerkyra to Messongi From 08.45 to 19.30, 2 hourly, 180drs.

— Kerkyra to Aghios Georgios (Argirades) 08.45, 12.00 and 17.30, 270drs.

— Kerkyra to Aghios Gordos 09.15, 14.30 and 17.30, 130drs.

Return tickets with a 10 per cent reduction can be purchased. Services are subject to alteration and the above information should be used as a guide only. Greatly reduced services operate on Sundays and holidays.

Taxis

There are taxi ranks in Kerkyra in the old port area, to coincide with ferry arrivals in the new port area, opposite the Old Fort in Douzmani Street and outside the airport. The vehicles have a dark navy paintwork with a white roof. All have meters.

Vehicle rental

All the resorts have arrangements for hiring vehicles of all kinds from the travel offices. Since their cut is taken out of the car hire company's fee, not added onto the price you pay, there is no incentive to hire direct from the car rental agencies.

In Kerkyra the car hire businesses are mostly in the new port area and the rent-a-bike offices are between the two ports.

Renting is an expensive business especially for cars.

Petrol stations

There are very few places where it is possible to go more than five kilometres without passing a petrol station and Kerkyra's approach roads are full of them. One spot where there is a shortage of stations is the area directly between Skripero and Roda.

Details of which petrol stations will operate the 24 hour service are given in the English language paper *The Corfu News* and broadcast on Radio Antenna in English at 22.00hrs. Most garages will have details and some may even post a notice in the window. The tourist police will have or be able to obtain this information as will ELPA. See Chapter 14.

Maps

There are no fewer than eleven different maps of Corfu on sale, and possibly more. The best for detail of villages and road conditions, but not infallible, is the one sold in the ELPA "portacabin" in the old port: published by the Efstathiadis Group. If you are going on to visit other Ionian Islands then it may be more economical to buy the Clyde Leisure Map of Corfu and The Ionian Islands. Like most Corfu-only maps, it includes a street plan of the town and a small map of Paxos. The free handout from the NTOG has small but useful maps of both the island and town.

THIRTEEN

Kerkyra

The town centre

Those arriving in Kerkyra will dock at either the old or the new port depending on the type of ship used. The international ferries use the newer port, which is shown on most of the maps as port number one. The smaller ferries that ply the route from Igoumenitsa dock at the old, or number two port to the east.

The harbour for the international ferries is in front of a suburb of the city called Mandouki and it is a largely residential area. Odos Xenofondos Stratigou, which links the two ports, curves round the bay past many restaurants and rent-a-bike businesses, while on the seaward side is limited mooring for the excursion boats and yachts. After 400m and at the foot of the hill that is the site of the New Fort — hidden except for some rich greenery and some steep walls — a fork branches off to the left and into the new port area.

The original road leads into a busy square where canopied cafés have a bright array of seating and tables under the plane trees. Still a pleasant location for a coffee, even though only a short distance away the traffic jam is building up, and impatient excursion buses hoot at the horse who under cover of his straw hat seems not to care at all and whose driver certainly has got used to that sort of thing years ago.

The buildings that front the square are most noticeably the large Agricultural Bank and the Constantinople and Acropol Hotels. From this area are three entrances into the maze of streets and alley ways beyond that form the old town. The coast road is first known as Donzelot and then Arseniou as it climbs past the court house, some travel offices, and two canopied pizza restaurants involved in an ongoing feud but where diners enjoy a tremendous view across to the mainland with Vidos island in the channel. The steps up to the Solomos and Byzantine art museums begin here, just before the first of the "stop" signs on corners where it is best to do as it bids

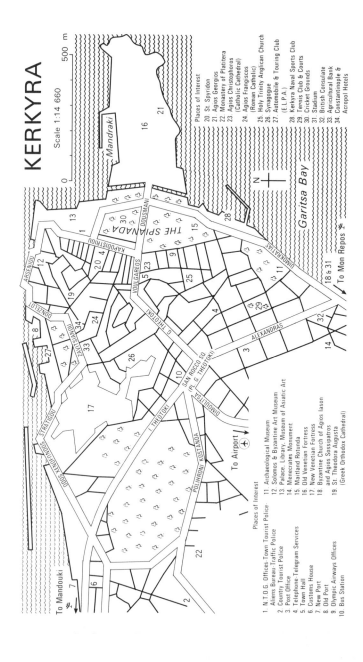

KERKYRA

Scale 1:14 660

0   500 m

Mandraki

THE SPIANADA

Garitsa Bay

N

To Mandouki

To Airport

To Mon Repos

Places of Interest

1. N.T.O.G. Offices Town Tourist Police-
   Aliens Bureau Traffic Police
2. Country Tourist Police
3. Post Office
4. Telephone Telegram Services
5. Town Hall
6. Customs House
7. New Port
8. Old Port
9. Olympic Airways Offices
10. Bus Station
11. Archaeological Museum
12. Solomos & Byzantine Art Museum
13. Palace, Library, Museum of Asiatic Art
14. Menecrates Monument
15. Maitland Rotunda
16. Old Venetian Fortress
17. New Venetian Fortress
18. Byzantine Church of Agios Iason
    and Agios Sossipatros
19. St. Theodora Augusta
    (Greek Orthodox Cathedral)

Places of Interest

20. St. Spyridon
21. Agios Georgios
22. Monastery of Platitera
23. Agios Christophoros
    (Catholic Cathedral)
24. Agios Frangiscos
    (Roman Catholic)
25. Holy Trinity Anglican Church
26. Synagogue
27. Automobile & Touring Club
    (E.L.P.A.)
28. Kerkyra Naval Sports Club
29. Tennis Club & Courts
30. Cricket Grounds
31. Stadium
32. British Consulate
33. Agricultural Bank
34. Constantinople &
    Acropol Hotels

Street names: ODOS XENOFONTOS, STRATIGOU, ARSENIOU, DONZELOT, KAPODISTRIOU, DOUSMANI, VOULGAREOS, G. THEOTOKI, SISSINI, KAPODISTRIOU, I. THEOTOKI, POLIHRONI KOSTANDA, DINOULISSA, SAN ROCCO SQ. (PL. G. THEOTOKI), ALEXANDRAS, DIMOKRATIAS you. The Reading Society is on the right and the traffic police on the left at the point where the road belatedly becomes one way. Its counterpart emerges disrespectfully from under the Arch of St Michael, which houses the entrance to the NTOG offices. Small well tended gardens front the Palace of St Michael and St George and continue along the perimeter road past the Guilford Memorial and on to the entrance to the Old Fort where Schulenburg's statue and a cannon keep guard.

The Spianada, a large lawned area, is divided into halves and the southern end is a shady park with benches dotted along the walkways and a bandstand that looks almost as incongruous as the Maitland rotunda, a columned basilica that marks the entrance to this park. The inner edge of this green oasis is bordered by what is probably Corfu's most famous thoroughfare, the Liston, which got its name from times when to be allowed to stroll its length you had to be high enough in society to have your name on the list of those permitted to saunter there. It is now lined by cafés, bars and eateries that are allowed to charge luxury prices for the benefit of such a pleasant location. Dozens of side streets lead off from here and the souvenir shops gradually give way to commercial shops.

San Rocco Square, also known as Platea G. Theotoki, where shops, one of the bus stations, banks, and a few cafés are located, is at the point where all roads seem to lead! One such route is Alexandras Avenue that leads to the perimeter road (now known as Dimokratias) and overlooks Garitsa Bay. It's a rather smelly area on most days but still an attractive bay with the Old Fort at one end and the little harbour at Anemomylos at the other. The tree lined coast road passes the luxury Corfu Palace Hotel and the turning up to the Archeological museum, before reaching the Mon Repos beach and then turning inland to wind up to Analipsis and Kanoni after having become one way again en route.

Kanoni

For centuries Kanoni has been a beauty spot but the changes that have taken place in this area have transformed it from a rural picnic spot to a fashionable address. Once covered in woodland, Kanoni now sprouts an assortment of expensive hotels, including the Hilton, apartment blocks, cafés and restaurants, which owe their existence to the marvellous view from there down to the twin islets of Pontikonissi and Vlacherna below. Pontikonissi, or Mouse

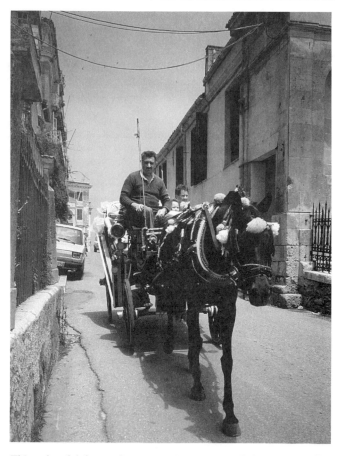

This colourful form of transport is seen around the town at all times of day and in all weathers. When it rains, the ornately decorated paintwork gets covered with a plastic sheet and the horse with a blanket and a knitted woolly hat.

Island, is an evergreen island with a mini Liechtenstein castle type church gleaming in contrast to the foliage. So photogenic is it that it has become the symbol of Corfu, appearing on all souvenirs and innumerable postcards. It is not a true island as it is joined to the mainland by a narrow causeway. Vlacherna has an equally appealing convent taking up nearly all of its surface and providing the ideal foreground to Pontikonissi beyond.

No more than ten metres further down hill, the view, though equally enthralling, has a totally different appeal: past the fish farm stick fence enclosures, Xalkiopoulos lagoon has the runway of Corfu's airport running into it like the deck of an aircraft carrier, and many people gather at the self service snack bar to watch the comings and goings.

The Old Fort

From all parts of the southern half of the coastal road in Kerkyra, the eye is drawn to the rocky promontory that houses the Old Fort — an island but for the bridge that links it to Kerkyra opposite the Spianada. The channel between the two areas of land is lined with walls of stone that look as sturdy today as when they were built by the Venetians to protect the inhabitants from the many raids by both pirates and Turks.

In the channel and at the tiny harbour of Mandraki at the northern edge there are moorings for many yachts and caiques. Once across the bridge the only thing worth seeing are the views of the mainland beyond the islet of Vidos. There are no signposts to explain either the history or the use of the buildings within the walls except for the offices of the market police and welfare pensions department.

All of the steep paths lead infuriatingly nowhere except to a locked gate at just the point where the trail looks to become interesting. Parents of small children should note that there are some uncovered wells with drops of 5m near the view points.

Even the former Anglican church of St George is locked; it is the building that looks like a fully intact Acropolis to the east and just within the gates. There is no admission fee except during the hours of the Sound and Light Show (see Chapter 20).

The intense green of the vegetation on Pontikonissi (Mouse Island) as seen from the balcony of a café at Perama. Some Greek tourists offered an alternative derivation of the name Pontikonissi as being from the word 'pondi' (centimetre), as the island is so small.

The New Fort

This has been described as disappointing and indeed they wouldn't let me in! It is now used as a Naval Base and the upper reaches are overgrown and said to be hazardous owing to the presence of snakes. I am not sure whether they were wearing uniform or not but, at least for the time being, these reptiles mean that the area is off limits except during Navy Day which no one is willing to divulge the date of. It wasn't even permitted to photograph the Lion of St Mark above the entrance in case it should enable the enemy, armed of course with this invaluable guide book, to locate the whereabouts of the establishment that hovers above the old port.

The British cemetery

The lines from Rupert Brooke's poem: "There is some corner of a foreign field that is forever England," came to mind as I walked amongst the tombstones in this haven of peace and tranquillity in the midst of a busy island's capital.

As you open the gate, a little bell announces your presence to the startled caretaker. The area inside is bursting with colour from the various flowers and shrubs that have been lovingly nurtured, and an incongruous shell mobile of Philippine origin hangs over the concrete pond unnoticed by the goldfish below who are probably more concerned with the precarious level of the water. There are, I am told, many rare species of orchid within the grounds.

The fact that the War Graves Commission sponsors the upkeep of the cemetery ensures that the graves will never disappear below a jungle of vegetation, but when you leave the area closest to the house, the plots are bare except for the most recent of sites, and the long strip of graves of the crew of two destroyers that were sunk in the channel off Corfu.

The smell of humus and damp are emotive. As you read the inscriptions on the headstones that tell of a young sailor killed in a practice exercise, or a list of new born children, eventually followed by their bereaved and long suffering mother in an untimely death, it is difficult not to be moved. If you can resist reading the headstones the visit need not be a depressing experience, and this is an excellent place to unwind. It is unlikely that the cemetery gate will be locked at the location signposted along the road opposite Dimolitsa, a turn-off from San Rocco Square that passes the asylum.

The memorial service at Lazaretto island where 143 men were executed by firing squad during the civil war for their political beliefs.

Vidos Island

People are discouraged from visiting this islet in an effort to minimise the risk of fires, and a team of boy scouts annually collect up the litter and flotsam that accumulate. Now inhabited only by a retired policeman, it was once the location of a reform school where the boys were allowed to roam free, confined only by the sea.

Vidos is the lonely setting for the Serbian cemetery where, after the first World War, the platoon of soldiers that died on Corfu of plague are buried. Until recently relatives of those buried here made the annual pilgrimage from their homeland but too many years have passed for there to be any survivors.

The island no one was ever happy to visit

Lazaretto islet, also known as Gouvion, was once a place of quarantine for ships carrying plague during the period of Venetian occupation. Its later role was much more horrific as it was here that executions were carried out during the civil war. Every 27th May, one of the smaller passenger ferries makes its annual pilgrimage to the island carrying hundreds of Corfiots who have just emerged from the memorial service in a nearby church.

All these citizens are communists or family of the young communist men that were shot. The prisoners were brought four or five at a time from the New Fort to Lazaretto by rowing boat and then stood up against the wall where now the bullet holes make poignant holders for the carnations placed by the families.

On this pilgrimage, the priest intoned the prayers and then from the balcony of one of the only two buildings there, a derelict house, two party officials read aloud the names of the 143 (documented) who were executed. Wreaths were placed by family members and then two letters were read aloud. They had been written by two of the young men immediately before their deaths, and the messages for their parents, wives and children were incredibly moving as they bid their wives to remarry and their children not to be consumed with bitterness towards the executioners.

Political and nationalistic songs were sung until a message from the captain urged us to hurry as the weather was worsening and the mooring was unsafe. We returned along the difficult path that took us the length of the island and onto the boat for the half-hour journey back to Kerkyra. Although the Mayor was present, the port police had denied all knowledge of the departure.

There are plans awaiting approval to build a petrol holding station on the island.

Architecture

Corfu and Paxos are more fortunate than their southern neighbours whose position along not one but two seismic fault lines has meant that they have suffered throughout their histories from earthquakes, the last of which in 1953 caused tremendous damage.

Because Kerkyra was a walled city, it grew within the protective boundaries in an upward direction as extra storeys were added to existing buildings in the same architectural style. This has had the result that many of the buildings look older than they really are. It is just as well that the foundation levels were of a sturdy construction as many have risen to four or more storeys and the original roof level can sometimes be seen in the remains of a tiled row on the facade.

Another factor that limited the direction of growth of the dwellings was the military desire to keep an area of open ground — the Spianada — between the Old Fort and the town so that should the latter fall into enemy hands, it was far enough away across an exposed area to pose no additional threat to the defences.

The overall effect of the style of the houses in the town is Italian if not Venetian, resulting in a very attractive town enhanced by an unusual amount of park land in and around the capital.

FOURTEEN

Useful information

Banks

There are two branches of the National Bank of Greece in Kerkyra. The head office is in the little square at the far end of G. Theotoki from San Rocco Square and the exchange desks are on the first floor. When they aren't on strike, they open from 08.00 to 13.30 Monday to Friday and 09.00 to 11.00 on Saturdays. A sub branch at the start of Mantsarou Street off San Rocco is open only on week days.

The familiar colour scheme identifies a large branch of Barclays Bank on the corner of San Rocco Square. Open from 08.00 to 13.30 Monday to Friday and 09.00 to 11.00 on Saturdays.

Most people change money at travel agents and hotels as outside the town there are no banks that carry out exchange transactions. The municipal information office will also change money. See below.

Post offices

The whole island only has one main post office despite a list of telephone numbers in the directory that are as long as your arm.

It is in Alexandrias Avenue, which runs from San Rocco Square to the obelisk on the coast road, and just two blocks down from the square, and it is easily identified by the people coming out of it with steam coming out of their ears.

The Poste Restante, philately and information counter is to the right where the sign in English has slipped and gone behind another in Greek. There probably won't be a clerk there however, and on Saturdays you are expected to join one of the other queues. All other services are dealt with at three windows in the hall to the right. Each window has a separate queue but so far no bookmaker is

This lady was kind enough to let me provide you with an example of what the head-dresses look like. They are made of a blue and white check cloth known as a podia (apron) and are used to keep the head warm in winter and shaded in summer, not for reasons of modesty or religious belief. Some of the women in the more remote villages do tug the lower corner across their mouths as they near you but it must be to hide a quiet giggle or two!

taking bets about which will get you served fastest. After having selected your queue you wait. When you eventually get to be in sight of the window, you have a 33.3 per cent chance of finding that you are in the line for parcels only. Any attempt to move into a similar position in one of the neighbouring queues will be met with with a closing of ranks fit to please any drill sergeant.

The windows dealing with all services except parcels have green signs above them while the parcels only sign is in yellow. Open from 07.30 to 20.00hrs Monday to Friday and possibly at weekends in the high season (but it hasn't been so in previous years).

There are portacabin post office branches at Paleokastritsa, Roda, Sidari, Ipsos and Benitses but they still hadn't opened by the middle of June.

There is a small sub post office in the grocers in Skripero which will be open from 07.30 to 15.00, Monday to Saturday.

Those needing stamps for postcards can buy them from the same place as the cards with a permitted surcharge of up to 10 per cent. Greece hasn't yet gone over to the system where inland and EEC destinations are at the same rate. The rate for cards and letters to the UK is 70drs.

Post boxes are pretty commonly seen attached to walls and are identified by their bright yellow paint work.

Telephone offices

There are two OTE buildings in Kerkyra but the main office isn't easy to find on foot and it's even harder to find a way of getting there by road without going the wrong way up a one way street. The best route for vehicles, and not a bad way for pedestrians either, is from San Rocco Square into the post office road, Alexandrias Avenue, and turn sharp left at the first corner. Second turning right takes you into the one way and 20m down on the left is the office.

There are eight booths of which two are for international calls and there are separate queues. The international booths are connected directly with the international network, and so avoid the problem usually faced in getting a line out of the country, which can otherwise be almost impossible during the summer months. No restrictions are placed on the hours during which you can make transfer charge calls but you wait a long time. This office is open from 07.00 to 24.00hrs, seven days per week despite popular rumours of a 24-hour service. There is a bizarre collection of international telephone catalogues and it could take some doing to track down the required volume: East Miami was in with the Italian editions.

The second office is at 78 Kapodistriou at the south end of the Liston near the Olympic airways office. Open from 08.00 to 22.00hrs daily.

Health matters

The emergency telephone number is 166 or 39403.

Corfu General Hospital is open 24 hours per day at Ioulias Andreadi Street, which is a continuation of Polihroni Kostanta, one of the roads from San Rocco. Tel. 30062.

Corfu clinic is a private clinic on the main road to Paleokastritsa in the Kapoutsinos area. Tel. 36044.

There is reputed to be a first aid centre behind the Commercial Bank of Greece in Skaramanga Square at the end of G. Theotoki Street off San Rocco. Tel. 39615.

The travel offices and hotels have details of local doctors and will usually help in calling them. There are rural clinics in Aghios Mattheos, Kavos, Lefkimi, Perivoli, Argirades, Kastellani and Gianades.

As on the mainland the address of the 24-hour chemist for that period is displayed in every chemist's window but only in Greek. The hospital will also have this information as may the police.

Police

The emergency telephone number is 100. The Tourist, Traffic and Aliens police offices are all in various parts of the Palace of St Michael and St George in Kerkyra. Tel. 30265.

Port police and customs
As you might expect, these offices are housed in the complex of buildings in the old port. Port police Tel. 32655.

ELPA

The Greek national motoring service, and the equivalent of our AA, has a bright yellow portacabin in the new port area of Kerkyra which opens from 07.00 to 23.00hrs. For the remaining eight hours an answering service puts messages through to the duty driver for breakdown calls; tel. 104.

Membership is approximately 15,000 drs per year which includes some insurance benefits as the organisation is now allied with the Interamerican group and helicopter emergency link up. They keep a supply of maps for Corfu, Greece and other European countries but they are not of their own production. The best of those on sale is the Efstathiadis group production, also available from some book shops.

Advice can be obtained as to the best routes from Greece to other European countries but only from ELPA's Athens branch: tel. 01 779 1615 ext 174. The only way of getting information regarding the condition of the island roads is to track down the breakdown vehicle drivers and then communicate with them.

Information

The Greek National Tourist Information office is under the west arch of the Palace of St Michael and St George in Kerkyra. Open from 07.30 to 17.00 Monday to Saturday and 09.00 to 14.00 Sundays. Tel. 39730.

The Municipal Information Office is just inside the port buildings and its opening hours are variable to coincide with the arrival of the international ferries. Tel. 36257

The British Consulate

The offices moved in 1988 and are still incorrectly shown on all the maps as being located at 11 Alexandras Avenue. Now located just opposite the Douglas Obelisk at 1 Menekratous, and distinguishable by the Union Jack and the coat of arms on the gate post. Open from 08.00 to 14.00 Mondays to Fridays. Tel. 30055.

The Consul, Pippa Hughes, is a charming woman whose air of quiet authority combines with her friendliness to give an overall impression that is exactly what this demanding role requires.

Would you want to be the representative of Her Majesty's Government in the preliminary hearing of the case of a lager lout who is charged with putting a compatriot in the hospital? Seeing the worst of the British on holiday, and in most cases in trouble of one sort or another, hasn't made her at all cynical, which must be no mean achievement.

Other of the consulate's duties involve the liaison with the Embassy in Athens regarding lost passports and the repatriation of those who come a cropper in accidents of one sort or another. The previous week had seen three British heart attack victims! While I was sitting in her office, Pippa Hughes calmly dealt with the paperwork for three lads who had hot wired a hire car and then written it off in a crash with another vehicle. Their passports had been impounded until they managed to find £2,700 from somewhere!

Routine work includes repatriation of accident victims, those who die on holiday, those for whom the easier access to alcohol brings on occult psychological illness, and the destitute.

Because of her fascination for Greece and its history, she completed the year long course that qualifies her in the highest level as a registered guide for Western Greece. Nothing like knowing your territory! Sadly her private venture of the "English bookshop" in Guilford has recently had to close owing to lack of support. Perhaps the thousand or so British winter residents who all mourned its passing wished that they had patronised it a bit more while they had the chance. The selection was certainly impressive.

Reading matter

Books
All of the resorts have a selection of paperbacks in English and German and you don't have to go far to find your favourite daily rag. The only shops selling non fiction and classics are in Kerkyra:
— Likoudis, 65 Eub. Voulgarios Street, tel. 39845. Not at first conspicuous although it is large enough; next door to the large National bank of Greece in the little square at the end of G. Theotoki, a road from San Rocco Square. They have a large selection of Penguin classics and reference books on local subjects but are not very helpful.
— Mastoras, 100 Palaologou Street, tel 31941. From the same square as above, in the second turning to the left while facing the

bank. A small but interesting selection.
— Soulis, 12 Eub Voulgarious Street, tel 37741. Opposite the bank as above. A larger than usual selection of paperbacks.

The Reading Society in Donezelot Street is for the use of members only and membership can only be obtained by being voted onto the list. The public library is housed in the Palace of St Michael and St George and contains about a hundred battered looking hard back adventure stories. Open from 10.00 to 13.00hrs Monday to Friday.

Newspapers

Nationally the most well known English language paper is the daily *Athens News,* which is a sober looking tabloid newspaper that occasionally has some sensational items of scandal. It costs 70drs. The *Athenian* is a monthly magazine with rather serious articles mostly relating to life in Greece costing 325drs. *Greece's Weekly,* at 250drs, is a strange concoction of economic articles, tourist information and financial statistics.

Locally since the *Corfu Sun* ceased publication there is only one free monthly: the *Corfu News* contains some useful information and interesting articles. *Epaphi,* which means "contact", is an interesting and humorous monthly that is unfortunately rather difficult to get hold of. It costs 250drs. Enquiries at 7 Donzelot Street, Kerkyra.

Radio

Two local radio stations broadcast in English. Radio Antenna 97.1FM at 22.00hrs gives news and details of which chemist and petrol station will be open all night. Radio Feakes 95.3FM between 15.00 and 17.00hrs has news and advertisements.

Animal welfare

Two excellent charities operate from England: the Greek Animal Welfare Organisation and the Hellenic Animal Welfare Society. Both do invaluable work in this country where the situation is best summarised by saying that the attitude to animals is different from our own. Should you come across a situation in which an animal requires help on Corfu, contact Mrs Kolla at 17 Dinou Theotaki,

Kerkyra, tel. 49100, 39663 or 37995. These hard working and brave representatives usually know the language and have the contacts and influence to help sort things out. Don't forget them on your Christmas charities list at Greek Animal Welfare Fund, 11 Lower Barn Road, Purley, Surrey CR81HY.

FIFTEEN

Around the island: the southern half

There are 209 villages on Corfu and I have visited all of them, clocking up 2,800kms in the process. It is unlikely that any holidaymaker will do the same, for it needs both time and the financial resources needed for hiring a private vehicle. This chapter, then, is designed to aid planning a route of the places that you would most enjoy seeing. Places not included below were unremarkable — it is after all unfair to expect there to be something special about every village on Corfu any more than any other region.

The following summaries have been organised in a round-the-clock-face order, from and back to Kerkyra.

In and around Gastouri

Just past the Bintzan Inn (which takes the prize for the least Greek-sounding name on the island) at Gastouri is a signpost that reads 3km to Aghi Deka and 3km to Kastelli along the left hand fork. Kastelli never appeared and, contrary to what the sign would have you believe, it is apparently down the right hand fork at the same junction. However, as promised, three kilometres further on is Aghi Deka (which means "Ten Saints"): a large newish village. Just before a pleasant café, a side road leads to the left and uphill (steeply) to Stavros and then Dafnata — though, as a local woman explained to me, it isn't as simple as that, since the area is also known as Haliata, Loukata, Makrata, Kornata and Homianata! Whatever you choose to call it, it is attractive, peaceful, has wonderful scenery and is friendly. There are rooms to rent and sitting outside the "Tasffffff" bar is a pleasant pastime (no, *you* ask what it means, I am not going to provide *all* the answers!). Inside and to the right is an unusually tasteful decor of black wood church pews covered with white Flokati rugs in a setting of rough walls and

CORFU
THE SOUTHERN HALF

Scale 1:340 000

0   5   10 km

For legend see inside front cover

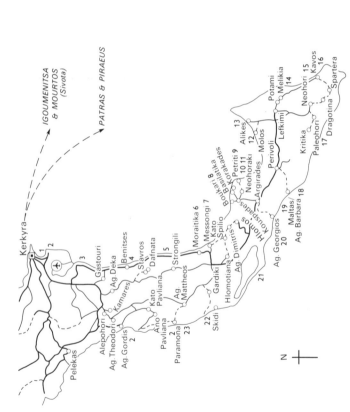

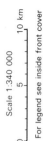

Index to Beaches

1. Garitsa
2. Mon Repos
3. Perama
4. Benitses
5. Ag. Ioannes
6. Moraitika
7. Messongi
8. Boukari
9. Petriti
10. Notos
11. Ag. Nikolaos
12. Molos
13. Alikes
14. Bouki
15. Kavos
16. Asprokavos
17. Kanula
18. Gardenios
19. Maltas
20. Ag. Georgios
21. Korission
22. Skidi
23. Prasouda
24. Paramona
25. Ag. Gordis

IGOUMENITSA
& MOURTOS
(Sivota)

PATRAS & PIRAEUS

Kerkyra

Pelekas
Alepohori
Ag. Theodoric
Ag. Gordis
Ano Pavliana
Kato Pavliana
Paramona
Skidi
Gardiki
Hlomotiana
Ag. Mattheos
Ag. Dimitris
Ag. Georgios
Gastouri
Ag. Deka
Kamares
Dafnata
Stavros
Strongili
Moraitika
Kato Spilio
Messongi
Boukari
Basilatika
Basvrakades
Ag. Barbara
Kounspadous
Neohoraki
Petriti
Argirades
Perivoli
Lefkimi
Kritika
Paleohori
Dragotina
Spartera
Potami
Melikia
Neohori
Kavos
Molos
Alikes
Benitses

N

an open fireplace; but to the left is a hideous bar, and space invader machines that for the first time made me sit down and think just what was meant by "space invasion" — and it has nothing to do with anything extra-terrestrial.

Back down to Stavros and on to Strongili where so few people pass by that you are greeted with the gesture that means "what are you searching for", as you *must* be lost to be there! After a few kilometres is a sign onwards to Ioannis Peristeron, John of the Doves, but either it doesn't exist or it is a deceptive name for that carefuly camouflaged "Club Med" site, and not having the assistance of the SAS I had no hope of gaining entry.

Benitses

Benitses is still described on some maps as being a small fishing village, which of course it was once. To envisage it that way today takes an awful lot of imagination, and it is now one of the largest and busiest resorts on the island. A small beach has been constructed here (yes, constructed) and shops, bars, fast food restaurants and discos line both sides of the road. The Kerkyra to Lefkimi route passes through this area, and not only is the flow of traffic obstructed but it is hazardous owing to the presence of a large number of hung over tourists doing silly things in the road.

The "Old village" is signposted but it just means that there is a larger proportion of clothes shops and travel offices set in narrower streets there.

Benitses ruins

Now you really must have a vivid imagination to be inspired by the ruins of a Roman villa just behind the bars of Benitses but here are the directions in case you should wish to see them as they are rather difficult to find without instructions. Between "Reflections" and "Black and White" bars is a very narrow alleyway. Follow it left and left again past the washing lines and then right at the fork and 20m on you will come to the wire fence around what might otherwise be a hazard.

Moraitika

This resort is similar to Benitses but scruffier and with a longer beach of the same type. Extensive road works were underway while I was there and everything was covered in dust, including me by the time I had passed through it.

Messongi

The border of what is sometimes shown as Mesongi or Messonghi and Moraitika is marked by the huge "Messonghi Beach" complex, where attractively lawned grounds containing two very large hotels and many chalets are surrounded by everything its visitors require during their holiday: a swimming pool, tennis courts (with tuition if desired), a piano bar, bingo, shops, hairdresser and a selection of restaurants.

The remainder of Messongi is fairly inoffensive as resorts go and in its favour is the fact that it doesn't parallel a major road. In fact it isn't signposted from anywhere, with the exception of a sign to the Seahorse camping site. The narrow road follows the path of a small, slow flowing river where even though the water is murky, the fish can be seen apparently enjoying the closed season.

Hlomos, Aghios Dimitris and Kato Spilio

One kilometre from Ano (upper) Messongi, a tiny turn off to the left leads up (and then down) one of the greenest hillsides on the island. The newly asphalted road twists at a rate that keeps you in a low gear both on the ascent and descent, but the patches of shade amongst the trees, and the views firstly of Lake Korission and then of the east coast as far as Messongi, make it an enjoyable route.

As soon as you enter the village of Hlomos, a primitive sign in English invites you further on and to the village of Aghios Dimitris. It is worth taking up this invitation as little worth seeing remains in Hlomos and the road that continues past the houses and then down is of a poorer condition than the advertised route.

In Aghios Dimitris are the well publicised "Taverna Tassos" and "Café 75 Steps Higher". I thought that the second part was information but it is the name of the establishment where pleasing decor and a mass of flowers provide an attractive setting from which

Greek people are amused when they see foreigners macabrely taking photographs of these little roadside memorials — the scene of an accident where someone was killed. Very occasionally you will see such a shrine to celebrate someone's near escape from death. Inside are placed an oilburning candle, a small icon and photograph of the deceased. Immediately after I had taken this shot my camera seized up for the day for no apparent reason.

to enjoy the view of the resort and other more natural sights below. Tassos has a pair of binoculars that you can borrow but my eyesight wasn't quite good enough for me to be able to make out whether the expression on the face of the paraglider was of pleasure or terror! For those who become addicted to this view, there are rooms and apartments to rent just further down the hill at Kato Spilio but nothing else of note.

Argirades

This is an attractive village at the place where the road to Petriti etc. branches off from the main route to Lefkimi. A convenient watering hole for those staying in Aghios Georgios who wish to see something Greek, there is a handful of tiny traditional cafés where you will have to use sign language for anything technical.

Petriti

The largest settlement in the group of villages (see below), this is an ideal base for those who want a holiday away from the crowds and with an emphasis on walking and eating rather than swimming and dancing. The beach here is pleasant enough despite an over abundance of seaweed floating about but there are plenty of other sandy stretches within easy reach. The village contains a few shops including the "Kalithea" supermarket, where metered telephone calls can be made, three restaurants and a small souvenir shop. For an evening venue, there is also a cocktail bar.

Basilatika, Boukari, Neohoraki, Korakades and Kouspades

Another pleasant little group of villages but these are more modern and apparently more prosperous than Sparterada etc. (see below). The other main difference is that they have made some contact with tourism, evident in the "Rooms to rent" signs and the advertisements for the inevitable fresh fish restaurants at Boukari and Notos.

From within the village of Argirades, a stack of signs points the way north and first reached is Neohoraki, modern and with little character. At Kouspades, the road divides with Basilatika and Boukari to the left, Petriti, Aghios Nikolaos and Notos to the right and a steep concrete slope straight on with a secondary route to Aghios Nicholaos, where the main attraction is a red café. Notos has very little beach but a disproportionate amount of rooms and small hotels.

Boukari is beautiful in its setting at the foot of the Hlomos mountain and the area has a verdant, peaceful and somehow healthy feel about it.

Geriatric coercion!

Anyone arriving at the waterfront in Boukari, whether by vehicle, on foot or by boat, is immediately pounced on by an enthusiastic octogenarian who very successfully persuades all comers into his fish taverna rather than the neighbouring establishment. The expressions on the faces of those he approached clearly showed their annoyance at attempts to herd them but they went along with it anyway! Handouts have been printed to give to customers likely to arrive by boat, advising them to insist that their captain drops them at his jetty rather than at any other. What a shame to have such untypical behaviour in such a lovely location.

Perivoli

The Argirades to Lefkimi road passes through Perivoli. I tried to like this village, even though the first time I passed through it was a Sunday morning and the whole village must just have come out of church. There were people standing about everywhere, all of whom looked hostile — a rare thing in Greece. I was struck by the incredibly high proportion of mentally retarded people and it was hard not to become melodramatic in my haste to move on. Scenes from the film *Endurance* came disconcertingly to mind and it is a feeling that I was to experience each time I passed through.

The road from Kerkyra reaches the village at the top of a steep incline, and immediately in front of the bell tower the road branches and "Murphy's Law" decrees that a tour bus will be coming from the opposite direction, causing you to veer violently to the right, which is where the signs to the beach point anyway!

One of the citizens of Lefkimi. She assured me that she didn't feel the heat in her many layers of widow's weeds although I was over hot in my T-shirt and shorts.

Lefkimi

Past the large and often helpful map displayed at the side of the road and the turn off to the health clinic, the outskirts of Lefkimi are pretty mediocre given the beauty of the majority of the landscapes of the southern edge of the island. The area is noticeably flatter than further north and much of the land appears to be disused, with the wrecks of cars and buses causing no obstruction.

Lefkimi is a town rather than a village and under the administration of its prefecture are Paxos and Antipaxos. There seems to be an over supply of yellow and white churches, all locked, and one of which, Aghios Arsenios with its twin bell towers, can be seen from all over the town.

As you approach from Kerkyra, you are immediately directed right and into a one way system where soon signs appear to Alikes, Molos and Kavos but none to the town centre. Turn right where more signposts for Neohorion and Kritikes join the choices. Continue straight along the main road, past a lighter than average yellow church, where the police station is immediately to the right of the sign to Kavos and the post office is just beyond to the left. Ahead, a small square is overlooked by an unusual church whose balconies give excellent views of the surrounding countryside.

The interior of Aghios Theodoros has an impressive ceiling and on my visit the atmosphere almost survived against the noise of the machines that were being used to grind the new floor of the sanctuary. The workers had conscientiously left their beer and cigarettes just outside the church door but they looked very incongruous on the steps. In the same square are a branch of the Agricultural Bank of Greece, three cafés and a general store.

Molos

You can follow the signs to Molos, which is just a few houses and a tiny taverna set in the olive groves. Mini agricultural plots edge an area that is only just beach as the sea comes up right to where the vegetation begins. The gradient is so gentle here that 100m out you would still only be up to your knees, but don't imagine tranquil, blue seas for there is a current, which means that a constant succession of lace edged ripples that couldn't be called waves by any stretch of the imagination pattern the surface of a rather brownish sea.

The rather splendid Aghios Arsenios is the best of many such churches in Lefkimi but it is the only one with twin bell towers. These can be seen from most parts of the town and so make an excellent landmark.

What must have been a haven for resourceful isolationists is about to experience a ghastly transformation. Attica Reisen have almost completed a 270 bed hotel here and so the days of peace are numbered.

Alikes

This word is plural and you will hear the area referred to as "Tis Alikes", the Salt Marshes. A small hillock of salt covered by a plastic sheet and a solemn row of rusted wagons are all that remains of a once thriving industry that sent sun dried salt from the shallow greenish basins all over the island

For one reason or another, Greece's membership of the EEC has forcibly closed the workings and now negotiations are going on between the land owners and the council, who hope to take over the area and introduce shrimp farms.

For the moment at least, the area is peaceful and the few houses that comprise the village enjoy a pleasant setting amongst flat forest land interspersed with flower filled marshes.

The village has three tavernas, one of which is intriguingly named "Kapsourokavouras: The Love Sick Crab", which is the nickname of the owner. The aforementioned gentleman informed me that there were 200 beds available to rent in the village but the mind boggles at where! The signs indicating Perekakis beach at the entrance to the village lead past a mini market to a large restaurant/hotel where the owner organises all the accommodation thereabouts. There is a discotheque "Victoria" that looks as if it doubles as a storehouse in the winter months. The beaches round about have dark grey sand and are unlikely to become crowded

The side roads are trails made by the hunters' vehicles and they are of a fairly good standard for dirt tracks and make pleasant walks except for the clouds of midges and the risk of being mistaken for game!

Potami, Melikia and Bouki

Potami (not to be confused with Potamos in the north) means river and is an apt enough name, as Potami and Melikia are on the west and east banks of a large lazy river at a point where it is crossed by a bridge whose much abused surface bounces as the tour buses pass

Quite suddenly you come across this lovely river at Potami.
Having crossed the groaning bridge you are free to look for
somewhere to park in order to explore the river — perhaps from
one of the tavernas on the banks. The caiques moored there
enjoy the sure protection of the high banks and no storm at sea
can pose a threat to them.

on their way to Kavos. Someone in Melikia has been resourceful
and various colours of roofing tile have been used to pave a small
square where old Victorian style street lamps add to the not
displeasing oddity of the overall effect.

Bouki consists of a few houses along the side of the track to the
left immediately after the bridge, and unless you are travelling on
foot, your progress past the customers enjoying the fare at one of
the riverside taverners will be met by irritated glares. The length of
the river is dotted with the charming sight of skeletal hulls amongst
clusters of wild flowers and concludes at a peaceful stretch of coast.

Kavos and Aghios Georgios

Both of these contain all you expect to find in a resort except style.
Aghios Georgios has the better beach where two sandy stretches are
broken by a small outcrop of rocks that provide something for the

snorkellers to look at. The little church that gave its name to what was once a village is the only building there that isn't totally without appeal.

Kavos should perhaps have been named "Kava" which means off licence, as, in deference to the average tourist's most pressing requirements, these shops outnumber even the fast food restaurants. The villas start at a distance of three kilometres from the heart of the resort and I wonder if the brochures are honest in their description of the location of the accommodation here as a good few of the visitors have small children and may not be pleased to have to push a pushchair that far to get to the disco each evening. These outskirts are quite rural and in complete contrast to the centre.

The southern villages

A secondary road leaves Kavos for Spartera and on it you reach the "Fantasia Fresh Fish Restaurant" just when you have started to believe that the route continues uphill forever, and about as far from the sea as it is possible to get on Corfu. They have chosen a small wooden replica of a boat to hang from their sign to get the fish connection across to those that perhaps can't read. They haven't for some reason attached a replica bed to indicate that accommodation is also available — maybe fearing it might be misinterpreted!

A little further uphill and you suddenly reach a T-junction on an incline that makes it very difficult to stop in time to make up your mind where exactly you want to go. Left and up continues on to Dragotina and Neohori (New village) while to the right and down leads to Neohori (yes, the same one), Paleohori (Old village) and Kritika (they don't *all* translate!). It isn't quite as simple as that, of course, and it isn't shown accurately on any of the maps but after the initial inadequacy at the aforementioned T-junction, the signposts are quite explicit.

All the villages in this area are charming but my vote goes to ∨ Kritika where the colours seemed brighter and the houses more ancient and quaint. Where the villages have rooms to rent, a sign is prominently placed (usually in German). In other circumstances, ask at the local café and a child who has been costing his parents a small fortune in language classes will be summoned and put to the ultimate test!

As if the route weren't confusing enough, the villages are jointly referred to as "Neohoria" (New villages) on some signposts.

From Paleohoria there are signposts to Kanula beach and this is the best route as the dirt road that leads there from Kavos is very steep and totally unsuited for all vehicles.

Maltas or Aghia Barbara

There are two approaches to this area of uncharacteristically wide reddish sand beach. The first is a turning immediately past the little kiosk as you leave Perivoli to go south. The second is signposted as leading to Marathias beach from the bell tower in Perivoli.

Building is underway and there are already rooms and apartments to let with at least three restaurants and two souvenir shops/mini markets.

Hlomotiana

Back now on the main road and returning to Kerkyra, beyond Argirades, is a turn off to Hlomotiana. As it isn't on the way to anywhere, those with transport are unlikely to visit this typical village, whose streets are so narrow that turning round to make the descent again is no easy feat.

Gardiki

Gardiki castle is the ancient looking building on the right hand side of the road to Aghios Mattheos, down the first turn off to Mesavrisi. A break in the wire fence allows you up the track to approach the Venetian fortress which, by the smell of it, now serves as a Venetian cattle shed at night. Although the walls and towers are well preserved, you have to be an enthusiast to be inspired by the site.

An almost equally ancient sign is disappearing completely from view in the undergrowth. Inspection reveals what can just be distinguished as Italian and Greek indicating the lake and fortress to the left. The other features arrowed on the sign are no longer in existence.

Skidi

Skidi is just one of many beaches between the edge of Lake Korission and Sinarades. Isolated coves at the bottom of cliff faces with varying degrees of inaccessibility as well as long sandy stretches of beach are to be found here, but vehicles must be abandoned a kilometre or two away from most of them as the tracks leading in the right direction turn gradually to sand and then to single track and eventually to a path wide enough only for the lizards and those on foot, often with nowhere for you to turn round.

Aghios Mattheos

This is the largest village on the island, the villagers assured me, at least as regards area if not population. They believe that they are the direct descendents of the labourers brought by the Byzantines to build the fort at Gardiki and who colonised the area above the present village. The bombings of the Second World War destroyed many of the dwellings on the higher ground and the desirability of closer proximity to the road has brought the settlement to its present day altitude.

The village is a patchwork of styles: from its outskirts, the typical modern characterless houses, then pleasant cafés in the shade of plane trees in a small square just off the main road, and then both shabby and well maintained houses in the upper village.

Heading north from the square take a turning up to the left from the main road. Here the narrow winding streets begin and leave you hunting for somewhere wide enough to park the bike in order to get your camera out. The dilapidated and the newly painted have equal appeal and there are enough faces full of character in the darkened doorways to provide Bertolucci with extras for at least one epic.

The church from which the village takes its name is in good condition and has the unusual features of a fountain in the courtyard, plus a war memorial, and a pensive-looking bronze bust of Yannis Yannoulis that bears the inscription of gratitude from the people of Serbia to the villagers, in both Greek and Serbian. In 1917 there was a regiment of Serbian soldiers camped in the area around the village and at least one of the old timers remembers being given a gift of dried rations as a small boy's treat. The unfortunate soldiers are still here in the graveyard on Vidos island, as plague claimed most of their lives. They believed that garlic would ward off the disease and stocks were completely used up in their attempts at self cure.

The village has a natural spring which was their only source of water for many years. They still receive water from the same source but now by a much less direct route. The hydraulic pumps at Gardiki draw the water upwards and send it both here and on to the capital. Having been encouraged to see the place where the spring surfaced and the housewives would gather to collect their supplies, I was rather disappointed to come across a three-sided cement hut covered in a design that turned it into a three dimensional political slogan. Just above the "well" is one of the tallest bell towers and to the left is the start of a dirt road that leads on to Aghios Mattheos monastery, 1½ hours walk away. Uninhabited now, the monastery is tended by two women from the village. On its name day, 6th August, and on Easter Monday, all the villagers make the journey for two days of festivities on foot as only the hardiest motorbikes can make the trip.

The livelihood of the people is from the olives and the four olive presses. Although there are no rooms to rent within the village, it deserves a closer inspection than permitted from the tour buses that pass through.

Paramona

This village is shown on the maps as Pendati but signposted locally as Paramona. I took an almost instant dislike to this settlement although I wasn't able to justify it until later when I was served with a totally inedible omelette that earned me the disgust of a very thin looking stray cat who didn't want to have anything to do with it either!

There are a few each of rooms, apartments, fish restaurants and cafés, all modern and with no character. After Aghios Mattheos the road deteriorates and care must be taken not to get a wheel in one of the deep cracks that the rain gouges into the track.

Ano and Kato Pavliana, and Aghios Theodori

The Pavlianes deserve a visit only because of the scenery encountered between them, where the island's wild flowers are in greatest abundance and their heavy fragrance fills the air.

Aghios Theodori is a pleasant village where the modern houses have some style for once and there are some attractive gardens.

Kamares and Alepohori

These are shown on the map as two separate settlements but the villagers say otherwise. If you visit at midday, the road will be strewn with the proverbial sleeping dogs in such numbers as to make you wonder if you too won't start feeling the effects of some invisible nerve gas at any moment, especially as there isn't a soul in sight. Have a look at the stone wall at the end of the tiny square. Near the top someone has painted either the words of a song or some rather public instructions to his loved one to meet him after leaving by the window when her parents had gone to sleep so that they could elope. Let's hope they made it!

Now do yourselves a favour and take my word for it that there is no continuing route and all the exits from the square are dead ends. If you insist on disbelieving me then you will sooner or later have to turn round outside a house where your presence will alarm one of those previously slumbering canines and all hell lets loose. An angry bark from one and whoosh, they are all awake, and, with nasty looking teeth, are rallying to the cause of defending the village and hence preventing your escape at all costs.

Aghios Gordis

This is a small resort that has got off to a big start as far as tourism is concerned in the enormous hotel of the same name whose facilities are strictly private.

Unusual in that it isn't a long narrow stretch of beach hugging a main road, this area is one of the most attractive on the west coast. The cone shaped rocky protuberance above the hotel and the cylindrical rock clinging to the cliffs away to the north bring a welcome relief from the typically flat landscape of many beaches.

A small, suspiciously brown, stream divides the beach into two halves but it has no odour, offensive or otherwise. Adjoining the beach are a few shops, tavernas and a diving school.

Pelekas

Pelekas seems to have appointed itself as one enormous tourist information centre for those whose holiday centres around the beaches of Ermones, Mirtiotissa and Glyfada. That isn't to say that there aren't also a number of bars and souvenir shops but the accommodation in villas, small hotels and rooms is on the outskirts and along the cool narrow roads that lead off to the various beaches.

Towards the top end of the village, the little windy road forks and to the left is Ermones, while to the right, after some bumps and twists, the road reaches the sunset bar where it must really be spectacular to watch the day's end. It adjoins what looks like a very grand house excellently renovated but is really a brand new hotel. This spot has excellent views of the surrounding area as far as the capital and the islets beyond. From the car park, a paved path leads up to the Kaiser's Seat, an observation tower where binoculars have been positioned enabling you to see clearly the ferries approaching from Italy and the planes standing on the runway.

Aghios Ioannes

Well, after hours spent searching, I can now claim to have solved the mystery of the missing youth hostel. No one knew what I was talking about and directed me to a nearby camping site; but as the hostel was marked on many of the maps, I relentlessly continued my search. The answer is that it was converted into a hotel some years ago.

SIXTEEN

Around the island: the northern half

West from Kerkyra

West from Kerkyra, the road leading towards Pelekas and Ermones passes through Alepou (Fox), before it leaves behind the dusty, suburban enterprises. The side road to Kombitsi, although not like anything from a Tolkien novel as the name might suggest, is worth a detour if only to pass through a little woodland shade after the commercial desert and the heat of the open roads on this stretch. The road to the village circles and rejoins the main road just a few kilometres from where you left it.

No such reason can be found to justify a side trip to Kanalia (or Aghia Eloussa as its residents and some of the maps call it).

The golf club at Ermones is well signposted until you actually reach the entrance, when a tiny sign on a large brown five barred gate marks the start of the driveway.

Mirtiotissa

The Mirtiotissa beach and monastery turn-off is marked by a small blue sign in Greek lettering and with a small cross to the left as you leave Glyfada for Ermones on the most westerly road.

Much more in need of a cablecar than Ermones, the beach is at the bottom of a horrendously steep dirt road that had me walking in a sideways shuffle. Even this worried the couple ahead, similarly engaged, who seemed to expect me to bowl into them having started an unstoppable slide. Somehow, there were two motorbikes at the bottom and not even of the Enduro variety, but it is quite possible that the monastery dogs let them past on an otherwise unavailable route. Had the beach been as secluded and lonely as is appropriate to the only official nudist beach on the island, it would have justified the crab-like descent and a pretty exhausting half hour's

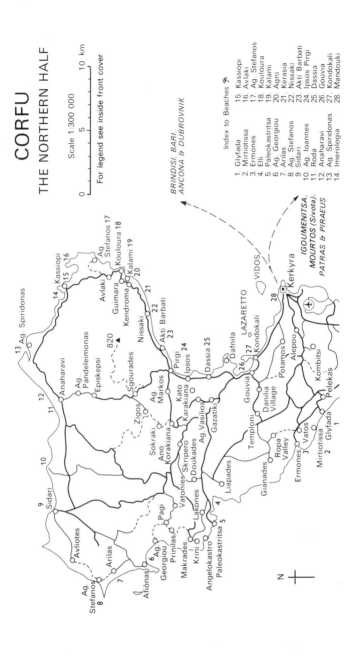

CORFU
THE NORTHERN HALF

Scale 1:300 000

0   5   10 km

For legend see inside front cover

Index to Beaches

1. Glyfada
2. Mirtiotissa
3. Ermones
4. Elli
5. Paleokastritsa
6. Ag. Georgiou
7. Arilas
8. Ag. Stefanos
9. Ag. Ioannes
10. Ag. Ioannes
11. Roda
12. Anaharavi
13. Ag. Spiridonas
14. Imerologia
15. Kassiopi
16. Avlaki
17. Ag. Stefanos
18. Kouloura
19. Kalami
20. Agni
21. Kerasia
22. Nissaki
23. Akti Barbati
24. Ipsos Pirgi
25. Dassia
26. Gouvia
27. Kondokali
28. Mandouki

BRINDISI, BARI,
ANCONA & DUBROVNIK

IGOUMENITSA,
MOURTOS (Sivota),
PATRAS & PIRAEUS

haul up again that manages to remove any benefits you feel from a refreshing dip; but the beach was the most crowded on the western coast and almost on a par with Kavos. When I started dressing to leave, a couple came and waited to park their towels where I had been.

It is sandy and with not a pebble in sight. A small amount of shade can be had from the boulders in the centre or from the men renting umbrellas. The beach is of the "breaker" variety — and body surfing is great fun — but it isn't of surf board standard. There are three refreshment stands and, worst of all, people with swim suits on! Some people have no consideration for others and I am sorry to say that this isn't the first time I have come across insensitivity of this type from people who have at least fifty other beaches to go to where bikinis are acceptable.

Although once described as being useful to rinse off salt at the end of the day, the natural spring that descends even quicker than you did is now only suitable for Chinese torture. Where the road reaches the sand, it immediately continues on and up the other side, past some soon-to-be rooms, to where 300m from the beach a water supply lorry was parked. Here stands the monastery of Mirtiotissa (turtledoves?) and a sign in English and German on the door advises visitors to the ring the bell — by means of that piece of stout wire hanging down to the left of the entrance.

Despite telling me that entry was forbidden during midday (1-5), I was admitted to what looked like any other Greek house and garden that just happened to have a church in the grounds. Going into the tiny chapel the difference between the brightness outside and the dimness within will have you almost blinded, and trying to make out something of the detail of the few "un-gold-encrusted" places on the icon is not easy! It sits on the right hand side of the iconostasis and was found as a result of a priestly vision where the location of the icon was revealed. The monastery was built as close to the site as the cliff face would allow. This is what I was told by the monk's brother-in-law but it isn't borne out by any account that I have found in print; and this gentleman neglected to mention that it was the original church that dates back 600 years and not the present day building, which was constructed to replace what was destroyed by a rock fall.

I was invited to buy one of the slices of wood that look as if they have been franked with a gilt painted stamp in a crucifix design, which I was told had been hand made by nuns. A few weeks later I was to meet one of the nuns who make these icons and she told me they bear a pressed on design.

No photographs are allowed inside and when two Americans arrived I was shoved around the back to see the bell tower. After getting lost in the vegetable patch, I found that it wasn't worth the film. Although the setting for this monastery is pretty enough, it isn't possible to photograph, or indeed see, the views from the grounds.

Glyfada

Glyfada is another small beach at the bottom of a steeply walled cove. Promises of facilities were not fulfilled, and at the grand Glyfada Beach Hotel the reception staff were unwilling to answer my enquiry as to whether the facilities were open to non residents so it seems unlikely somehow. The Top sail club complex was completely deserted even though the doors were open. I did actually manage to get a coffee at the taverna café at the northern edge of the beach. The last 200m of the approach road is steep and unsurfaced.

Vatos

Vatos is shown on the maps as a village 2km or so up the hillside from the road between Ermones and Pelekas, and with only one road leading to it, but that isn't the case. The road circles and rejoins the original highway further towards Ermones. A small unremarkable village, its name was taken for the camping site that is located one kilometre from the turn-off up to the village.

Ermones

Organised around a comparatively small but beautiful cliff-edged sandy beach, this little resort has everything for those who want an energetic holiday; and those who wish to laze around could find their consciences being irritated by all those divers, skiers, sailors, volleyball players and canoeists who enjoy an activities-centre beach.

This location is convenient for those whose holiday centres around the golf club, as it is only 3kms away and therefore much nearer than Glyfada. Far enough above the beach not to spoil the area, the large Ermones Beach Hotel seems at first to be one enormous building with extensive gardens. On closer inspection it is revealed as a complex of bungalows with vegetation in between and reception and tennis courts at the top of a long winding drive-way. For those who don't wish to end a day at the beach with an uphill ramble to get to their rooms, there is, would you believe, a cable car to take you to the appropriate level. Just press the bell and it comes straight away! The four tennis courts are open to the public but the other facilities are private.

Ropa Valley

After the hills and mountains of the south of the island with its dark greens and musty shade, the valley with its cornfields and wide open spaces comes as a bit of a shock, though by no means an unpleasant one. I found myself marvelling rather uncharitably that an airport hadn't been built here! The stretch of new road that crossed the plain and the gentle breeze were enjoyable and I made a point of repeating the experience.

Gianades

Gianades was rather a disappointment as it has been described as a gem of a village. I entered by way of Temploni and came to a signpost pointing right to Marmaro and Kanakades and left to Gianades. A short distance further on, the road again divided with no clue as to which was the correct road. The right hand branch offered further choices half a kilometre later: to the left was the option of going to Sianades that later became Samouna, and a sign to "The centre" led me up a tortuously steep slope into someone's back yard with no viable reason why.

For those who don't like making decisions, Gianades, when you eventually find it, poses problems, as every 50m there is a turn off with a signpost to what might be a village to local people but is best thought of as being a street. It isn't an ugly village but neither is it one of the prettiest, and it has nothing to distinguish it from many others. Marmaro below was as pretty as Kanakades was ugly.

Liapades and Elli beach

On the main approach road to Paleokastritsa from the south, Liapades can be seen perched proudly on the hillside and the effect of the mottled, ageing ceramic roof tiles is a pleasing contrast to the green of the surrounding countryside. Once you begin the ascent into the village, however, the effect is lost, all the more so if you are in a vehicle as the road is steep and very narrow, so you tend to keep your eyes on the road and your mind on what might be coming around the next corner. Even for passengers, the effect is lost when seen from street height.

Just inside the start of the village, the road forks and the branch to the right descends to Elli beach. This comes as a suprise, as you will have passed many usual tacky tourist traps and may be forgiven for expecting to find another "towel edge to sunbed edge" resort at the end of the route. Yet here, although the "Elli Beach Hotel" is of the usual unimaginative architecture, the beach is uncrowded.

Representatives for the speed boat, pedalo and canoe hire can be found (usually asleep) under an umbrella or makeshift shelter. There is also a service with a motor caique that holds 10 people and makes the 30-minute trip to the furthest of six secluded beaches that can be reached only by sea. En route you are shown the Galazia Mati or Blue Eye cave. The hire of the boat is 2,500drs for immediate return or 4,000 if you want to be dropped off at one of the beaches (to be collected again at a prearranged time). In view of the fact that the boatman likes his sleep, it might be as well to advise someone responsible of your intentions and to take food, water and a woolly with you, if not a helicopter.

The Elli beach is a small sandy cove bordered by cliffs. Breakers splash amongst the large smooth rocks that form channels and pools with the land at the northern edge. There are stones along the upper edge but the beach is of coarse sand.

Opposite top: *Gardens of the villas at Vigla whose occupants enjoy an unrivalled view of the Greek and Albanian mainlands.*

Opposite bottom: *The gorse that covers whole hillsides in a blanket of yellow during the spring and early summer seen here at Aghios Stefanos on the west coast.*

Overleaf: *An English family at Kouloura setting off for a day afloat. I haven't made a mistake, the caique is double prowed.*

Doukades and Skripero

I was hoping that Doukades would be quaint and traditional so that I could recommend it as somewhere for those staying at Paleokastritsa to visit in order to see something Greek. In the tiny village square I was confronted by a little sign pointing, it claimed, to Sidari and Skripero. I took the other turning and came to Skripero anyway! This village is large enough to boast a post office and, as you pass along a fairly uninspiring main road, there are occasional glimpses of the village otherwise concealed down from the side of the thoroughfare. The narrowest of roads gets even closer to the sides of a steep mountain above and you wonder if it is going to start the familiar zig-zag up to some lofty settlement just before it reaches the same sign.

From the right hand side of this high street, a road discreetly announcing itself as 10T descended and after a lovely route of nothing but rich countryside, it joined the main Paleokastritsa to Kerkyra road where once again it proclaimed 10T just past some chevrons.

This quiet café isn't as peaceful a location as you might imagine as it is on the route from Paleokastritsa to Lakones and a steady stream of tour buses pass by taking trippers to the vantage points.

Lakones

Poor Lakones must be dizzy from all the comings and goings via its one narrow street. Walls of buildings bear the scars of where buses, coaches and cars have taken a chunk of brick and left some paint in exchange as they try to get out of the way of another vehicle. Nevertheless the village is pretty and the old folk who sit outside the *cafenion* each afternoon still have enough bonhomie to wave at anyone who smiles at them.

At the upper reaches begin the competing claims to have the best view down to Paleokastritsa and a variety of exotic foods are advertised to help win more of the customers. You may have decided to order beef stroganof and sangria but when the waiter appears it will be regretted that those particular items are "off" today and it looks like moussaka and retsina again. Many of the restaurants are expensive here while others advertise that they charge "normal" prices.

Paleokastritsa

This must be easily the most visited village on the island, owing to the picturesque qualities of the coves on either side of an isthmus beyond which is a rocky outcrop, the location of the Monastery of The Assumption of the Virgin of the Old Castle. To my mind the area is no more beautiful than many others on the island and the ridiculous number of people crammed into such small beaches nearly completely covers the sand. The resort is divided into two bays, Alipa and Aghios Spiridon, both of which have an over abundance of hotels and tacky tourist traps.

It is said that Sir Frederick Adam, when High Commissioner, took a fancy to the area as a favourite picnic spot. As a convenient way of getting the route there surfaced, he declared the need for a road to link Kerkyra and a planned convalescent home at Paleokastritsa (the home was never built). The soldiers began grudgingly to construct the highway that is the pride of the island's roads.

Paleokastritsa is notoriously expensive both for accommodation and food in comparison with other resorts.

Krini and Angelokastro

Krini perches on top of the hill that also seats Lakones, and ... the top amongst the stalls of lace and rug sellers are signs to Angelokastro which direct you through some side streets and an olive grove to where the road becomes impassable. When you walk a little further on you come to realise that Angelokastro is in fact on the top of the neighbouring peak and, bearing in mind the angle of ascent involved, it is probably a good five hours hike and several dozen pitons away. From the same location you can see it clearly enough to appreciate that from the summit the castle really did have an all encompassing view, as far as the citadel in Kerkyra which looked to Angelokastro for early warning of attacks from the sea.

Makrades

This is approached either by continuing the ascent from above Lakones or from the road between Skripero and Roda. The village is small and scruffy with a collection of people by the side of the road who are intent on getting you to buy something.

The distance between Makrades and Vistonas looks nothing on the map but is deceptive, as the road is one long length of switch-back curves passing through some beautiful mountain ridges covered with a blanket of gorse bloom in spring and early summer. A café at Vistonas, one of the few buildings there, provides a welcome refresher after a challenging route.

Vatonies, Pagi and Prinilas

Vatonies is left almost as soon as it is reached but may catch your attention if only because it isn't mentioned on the signpost at the turn off from the road to Sidari.

Pagi has at its centre the fork where the tarmac road leads on to Aghios Georgiou (St George's) beach 2½ km away. The left branch goes on and up to Prinilas, a pretty, sleepy little village reached by way of a winding road where the clusters of Campanula are particularly vivid. In the area that serves as the village square, three routes leave: to the left is a poorly surfaced road that goes to Vistonas and connects with the Paleokastritsa area, but it shouldn't be a route of choice. The other two exits are dead ends.

Aghios Georgiou

Three roads lead to this small resort, the most northerly is from
Afionas and the part of the cove that it reaches has no connection
with the other two or indeed with the southern half of the gulf there.
Ten metres past the Golden beach hotel, a dirt road goes up to
Dafni and from there connects with the main routes. The last route
is the most suitable for everyone except cyclists and pedestrians (it
is steep) and it leads to Pagi.

Afionas

Two kilometres past the turn off to Aghios Georgiou, the ascending
road brings you to the village of Afionas, whose sign is rapidly
disappearing under the branches of a tree. The ascent is gentle
except for one nasty corner and suddenly there is a choice of left or
right. Left says something about St Georges and right continues into
the village. From where the trail ends and no parking signs
obviously want you to keep moving, a wide path to the right leads
down to a point where you can see an isthmus with a cove on either
side, before it broadens again and is the base for a lighthouse.

*Aghios Stefanos, one of two villages of that name that
coincidentally both occupy extreme geographical positions on the
west and east coasts. This is the latter of the two where there
are some rooms to be found in what is a small resort on a
beautiful cove.*

Aghios Stefanos

Not to be confused with the village of the same name on the north east coast, what looks to be a small village on the maps is a budding resort with building underway, and there is already a plentiful supply of restaurants, shops, and villas with the skeleton of a large hotel looming ominously in the background awaiting life.

While all the facilities are there, they are scattered along the turns and straights of a road that first ascends to Arilas and then descends to Avliotes. The beach is sandy but has a seaweed problem that they were attending to with the use of a JCB.

Arilas

The few advertisements that act as signposts to the beach from the road that passes through this sparse village don't prepare you for the busy little sea front found there. You can imagine that it was once someone's much beloved "one taverna beach" even though the businesses are quite tastefully designed. This is a popular area for wind surfers, but for those who have their own equipment rather than those wishing to hire or have lessons. When the sun sets behind the rocky ridge of Krava in the sea beyond it is a very pleasant sight indeed.

Avliotes

Avliotes is a fairly typical village whose approaches rise and fall, passing a hillside of cyprus trees so closely packed that they look like an evergreen wall. Weather worn signs pointing to "Sunset bar" lead the way to a pretty sandy beach at the bottom of a long flight of steps at the end of the concrete road.

Sidari

Small as resorts go and with a certain style, the unusual feature of this area is the sandstone that constructs the cliff face. Making a pleasant change from sandy strips of varying length that are the usual coastal landscape, gulleys and mini canyons have been formed where the sapphire sea has worn the yellow stone smooth except for

Two such lumps are all that remain of the 'Channel of Love' at Sidari. The elements have worn away the sandstone so, alas, the tradition what whoever swam between them whilst they were in shade, would achieve their heart's desire must remain only a legend.

horizontal ripples, and this provides both many individual coves for greater privacy and areas of perfectly flat (though sometimes tilted) rock to stretch out on.

Because of the permeability of the rocks, the postcards showing the "Channel of Love" will soon be collectors' items. Local folklore had it that anyone swimming the channel between two particularly large rocky promontories while it was in shade would forever be lucky in love. It is now difficult to differentiate the two masses concerned from all the others in the area. I must confess to disbelieving one taverna owner who told me that they were right in front of me and I searched the surrounding area in vain. Sidari can be seen in the near distance from the sandy, seaweed strewn beaches of Agnos and Astrakeri to the east. From Aghios Ioannis beach the dirt track behind the beach almost reaches there before it gives way to sand.

The church of Aghios Spiridonas, the island's patron saint, whose relics are marched around the town four times a year in gratitude for the miracles he has performed.

Anaharavi

This is a medium sized resort situated on the main road and with at least four parallel turn-offs to the beach with varying degrees of remoteness and therefore of crowdedness. There is the usual collection of shops, bars, travel offices and restaurants but most of the accommodation seems to be centred between the road and the beach, which is the long thin sort with a generous sprinkle of sunbeds. The seas are of the small-medium wave type, thanks to the north wind. The more isolated edges of the beach are quite lonely and lone bathers should be aware that there is a shepherd in the area with some nasty habits.

Aghios Spiridonas

The village is signposted from the main road in two places that later link up before proceeding down to a small stone and sand beach where there is a rather steep sub sea shelf. There are many other dirt roads leading off to villas but I followed at least eight and can confirm that they don't lead to any other beaches. The brown signs are to an olive press with a guard dog.

There are travel agents/supermarket, two bars and tavernas en route to the beach in a very isolated spot and where you would least expect to come across such things.

On this section of coastline between Aghios Spiridonas and Kassiopi are many places for those who seek an isolated cove from which to swim. They aren't easy to get to however and perhaps that is just as well.

Imerologia

Within sight of Kassiopi is Imerologia (Calendar) beach where the rocky outcrops to the north provide some degree of shelter to the pebbly coves, and enable wind surfing. A small harbour with the usually colourful caiques gives the area some character.

Kassiopi

Once a quiet fishing village, Kassiopi attracted the development that goes to make a fair sized resort and it is now difficult to picture it as it must have been originally. Atypical in that it looks more attractive from the seaward side than from the land, there are the usual tacky tourist traps that stretch from the village square to the sea and along the sea front.

The village becomes quite deserted at peak sunbathing hours as the beaches are all far west or east of the port. The former is reached by means of a footpath that leads past some lace shops and the ruins of a Venetian castle and fortress and on to a small sandy beach with numerous flat rocks where just about enough space is found for everyone to pitch their towels. Because the bathing areas are more exposed to the elements than other resorts, there is less of a selection of water sports available until you go west to Imerologia.

Kassiopi was of considerable strategic importance to its various occupiers, since whoever held Kassiopi held the channel between Corfu and Albania, and therefore controlled the trade route.

Avlaki

From the turning signposted just before Kassiopi (coming from Kerkyra), after passing a few bars and a travel agents, a dirt road leads down to a rocky, bath-towel size beach. The same name is given to another beach just around the corner where both the beach and the stones are larger. The road from here to Aghios Stefanos has been improved, which at the moment means that it is a wide and smooth dirt road until the first heavy rain or until it is sealed, whichever happens soonest.

Aghios Stefanos

It is quite a coincidence that both villages of this name occupy extreme geographical positions. This particular Aghios Stefanos is located at the point on the island closest to Albania just 1.7km away and visible through a varying amount of haze.

It's a beautiful fishing hamlet now with a smattering of villas, bars and souvenir shops in case anyone goes into shock at going more than 3km without seeing one. The road down is asphalted but rather steeply winding. The sea at this point is divided into three theoretical sections: 1km are Greek waters, ½km are International waters and the remainder is for the Albanians. The area of Albania seen clearest from here is the mouth of the river estuary at Exomilia where the mud flats and outline of the town can just be discerned.

Kalami and Kouloura

Dangerously photogenic, these two coves must have caused many near misses on the roadway above. You catch a glimpse in a brief

Excursion boats circling the bay at Kalami and no doubt pointing out the White House where Lawrence Durrell wrote 'Prospero's Cell'.

gap in the undergrowth and the scene is burned into the reti
an unguarded look at the sun, the vividness of the colour scheme
makes such an impression and your foot makes its own way to the
brakes. If you are northward bound then there is no problem as the
turnoff is reached after your first exposure.

One and two kilometres respectively from the main road,
Kouloura and Kalami are two of the most beautiful coves I have
ever seen and Paleokastritsa pales in comparison. If your only
glimpse of them is from a boat you won't agree, as the different
colours of the sea aren't visible, and even when you descend to the
shoreline, some of the effect is lost.

Kouloura, I am told, is the smallest village on the island with just
three houses. The large white house on the rocks there is reported
to have been owned until recently by the manager of Juventus
football team and Mr Fiat — but this is not true and only a distant
relation was involved. The same house has a brass plaque on the
wall which commemorates the visit of King George. I can't be more
specific as the owner seemed to have forgotten the details.

The word "Kouloura" means a type of biscuit that keeps for
months and is ring shaped. The bay is fairly round, as is the tiny
harbour wall that encloses many small caiques and provides even
better protection than the bay alone. A small pebble beach separates
the emerald from the sapphire: the woods from the seas.

Kalami is a small villa type resort whose facilities have so far
shown some discretion in their standards. A coarse sand beach edges
the small settlement where, as long as you don't want to paint the
town red in the evenings, there is everything you need for a quiet
holiday. It isn't as peaceful now as when Lawrence Durrell wrote
Prospero's Cell in the white house on the southern end of the bay.
Some renovations have changed the interior, which is leased by a
villa holiday company, but the outside is the same as when he lived
and wrote there, often in the company of Henry Miller.

Kendroma

This village north from Nissaki deserves better than to be called a
"black spot" but, as far as road accidents are concerned, it must
be. The already none too wide highway drastically narrows at this
point and the sides of buildings like the community office and the
police station border one edge, and a sheer drop the other. Just
before the café, there is a corner where even though you are going

slowly and have no intention of going there, the camber and tightness of the curve send you into the middle of the road and into the path of whatever is coming from the other direction. For these reasons the village is better appreciated on foot.

Guimari

Sounding more Italian than Greek, this village advertises a bakery from where it sits behind an attractive little church on the corner. Through the village are the footpaths that lead to Agni and Kerasia beaches which are frequent stopping points for the tour boats.

Nissaki

The fates and the village community were all against me when I came to view the beaches of this quiet villa resort. Two roads are signposted down to the shoreline announcing "Nissaki village community— Free access to the beach" but ten yards along the first road led slap into a five barred gate and the second ended up in someone's back yard. This was how it first appeared to me until I eventually worked out that the indicated routes were footpaths that you had already passed by the time you spotted the polite signs (the road here is full of curves and bends). They were even devious enough to place one at the entrance to a Club Med driveway and hence I had plenty of help from the two guards in manoeuvring my bike (it had stalled — probably in panic) back up the 1 in 2 gradient. The main road isn't short of turnings off in the direction of the sea where you know that there must at least be a rock to swim from, but all of them end up in the grounds of villas with locked gates or private houses with guard dogs.

Where you come to the Nissaki Beach Supermarket just down from the main road, the turn-off continues down to a small inviting cove with two tavernas, two souvenir shops and a travel office where Judy, a delightful English woman with twenty years on the island, is very wiling to give expert help and advice to anyone who should seek it.

Souvenirs

Anxious to keep within my budget and conscious of the amount of junk already taking up every inch of storage space to the point of displacing the kids in our little house, it was a relief to find myself totally uninspired by the souvenirs displayed in all the shops on the island. I am not aware of the fashion trends in the UK of late but if the clothes racks in Corfu are anything to go by, then ROSPA must be delighted by the decrease in the number of nightly road accidents, as everything from hairbands to sunbeds, from toothbrushes to underwear, is phosphorescent. The manufacturers have obviously formed the opinion that it "won't go if it doesn't glow" in either pink, lemon, green or day glow orange.

It wasn't until I got to Nissaki and eventually found a way down to the beach that I came under temptation. A sign reading "The Loom" and a traditional rug at a bargain price were enough to get me up the steps to look at the displays both inside and outside the little shop that seemed to specialise in rugs and pottery. When I complimented the owners — a French-Canadian woman and her Greek husband — on the high quality of everything on display, they explained their aim of collecting together handmade items from all over Greece that are not generally found in Corfu. This they had certainly achieved and when they pointed out their "up the stairwell" display of exquisitely decorated china and mirrors, I knew I was going to have to lighten my purse a bit before I left.

Akti Barbati

The first time I went to this comparatively quiet stretch was by way of the road that was marked by a decapitated sign that read "AY TO THE EACH". The next day when I passed by the sign was in a neighbouring field, hence providing a good example of the impermanence of such landmarks and the consequent difficulty faced at times by guidebook writers. Now I can only suggest that you look out for the large metal water supply tank that the lorry driver had left hanging from a tree (yes, really) just down the side road; or alternatively take the well advertised turning 300m further on. The first route is cobbled with large and slippery stones and makes treacherous going for its 400m length. Those going by bike should firmly secure their baggage and passengers as, unless the suspension on your vehicle is completely non existent, you will bounce down rather than drive.

A taverna here has live entertainment in the evenings while paragliding and other watersports are available at the pebbly water's edge where the trees make it a more attractive beach than the resorts to the north. Should you disagree, a sea taxi will take you to Ipsos for 200drs.

Ipsos

With less class than nearby Dassia, this resort is reminiscent of Kavos and Benitses but with only the landward edge of the beach road being packed with the usual amenities.

Most of the night life is centred in the middle with the two ends being the quieter areas. The three camping grounds serve the demand for low budget accommodation including the "Paradise" where the practice of painting the trunks of trees white to deter pests has taken a bizarre turn — thirty or so treetrunks in an otherwise attractive field have been painted sky blue, which looks AWFUL!

I sampled the delights of "Al's Plaice" (fish and chip parlour) and can confirm that they were just like those back home. I am told that the English breakfast here is the best in town, by customers that claimed to have tried them all! The same couple, my fellow countrymen, were there for seven nights and had three more to go and were lamenting how little there was to do. They were grateful that they weren't on a two week holiday even though the weather was fine and every shop and business was open except the waterslide. The fact that there was only lager and no bitter beer on sale was lamented plus the fact that there were so few people.

There seems to be no dividing line between Ipsos and Pirgi but the latter generally refers to the northern edge of the strip of beach entirely covered by small grade shingle that is raked flat and clean every morning to provide a level base for the sunbeds.

Sun bed hire

The price of sunbeds is by no means a standard thing whether it legally should be or not. In most cases, the owner or his agent don't appear until midday when enough people will have taken them up on the "help yourself" signs. The price is then set by what they estimate to be your experience or lack of it as to what the correct going rate is, which they cleverly determine in direct proportion to how tanned you already are! Lily whites beware!

Aghios Markos to Episkepsi

Between Ipsos and Dassia on a wide but tricky road section, an inland turn off adjoins the main route exactly on a bend half way up a very steep hill. If you are ascending it's on the opposite side of the road which makes it difficult to turn into. On its own Aghios Markos is hardly worth the effort unless you are planning to call in at the Paradise bar and sample the local brew — which, unlike the cocktails in the resorts below, at least admits to being a close cousin to wood stripper.

Kato Korakiana, Aghios Vasilios and Gazatika are all pretty unremarkable but the delightfully scruffy Ano Korakiana is worth a visit. Here the only sign in English was a rough translation of a plaque in Greek that read: "In this house lived and created his great work of art the first self taught popular from Corfu sculptor; Aristides Zach. Metallinos". High on the side of a house that was only distinguishable from its neighbours by being more recently painted were both the plaque and a small balcony which was full of rather atypical statues. The most immediately noticeable was of a female figure just about wearing a dress of which one button is done up at waist level and which must have shrunk considerably in the wash.

Unwittingly I continued along a well surfaced route that is shown on the maps as having a bend or two along its length. I wish I had started counting at the start as there were anything between 15 and 20 hairpin bends before it reached Sokraki, where the villagers looked very surprised that I had bothered to make the trip — and having looked around, so was I! Zigos was less of a challenge to reach and the road has now been completely surfaced in contradiction to many of the maps. In fact it has even had time to develop a pot hole or two in the asphalt.

Sgourades is a narrowing in the road with a house or two and a little shop. North and on to Episkepsi, meaning visit, and it is worth a visit for the colour scheme of the house fronts. Suprisingly, there is no petrol station and so I can vouch for the fact that the road from Episkepsi to Anaharavi is all down hill, because I coasted the entire length of it and was pleased to be greeted by a BP sign at the bottom, even if it was a kilometre away to the west. Along the route I had passed signs informing me that I was first entering, and then leaving, Aghios Pandeleimonas with only a tiny group of houses in between. The signs along the Kassiopi—Roda road, pointing to

Aghios Pandeleimonas and to the petrol station, are the only markers at the start of this route.

Dassia

Well, if resorts have to be on such a large scale, at least put them where there is some scenery for the visitors to enjoy and put them out of sight of the rest of the world.

This is fortunately the case at Dassia. Once more on the coastal road and continuing south, a gradual build-up of souvenir shops and fast food restaurants begins with The Chandris Palace hotels sitting contemptuously in the middle (their facilities are private). The road is atypically wide enough to cope with the flow of both traffic and pedestrians, the latter usually heading eventually down one of the many side roads which lead to a very narrow long sandy beach, where several piers have been built to give bases to the various water sports centres that compete for customers.

At the far northern end of the beach, multinational signs inform you that the remainder of the beach is private property, as are the water polo, tennis, volleyball, football and basketball courts there. Yes, you've guessed, it is a Club Med! The entrance to this bamboo hut type village is 300m further north on the main road, not that the knowledge will do you much good.

Back on the main road, the next seaward turn off is to Paradise beach where 800m further on a tiny pebble beach with some facilities can be found.

Dafnila

Passing Dionissos camping on your left, the hillside and its greenery fortunately hide from view the grand Astir Palace and the ugly Eva Palace hotels, the only eyesore in this otherwise attractive, verdant landscape that is reminiscent of Yugoslavian scenes.

A few rooms, a handful of small hotels, a spatter of restaurants and a couple of music bars have not so far intruded on the peaceful atmosphere there but unfortunately the stretches of beach are few and small.

This area can be reached from either the north or south as the routes join along a sub-road. From the north follow the signs to the Astir and Eva Palace hotels and then through a small network of narrow streets. The flow of traffic here is regulated by traffic lights that leave you sitting wondering if perhaps you aren't the subject of a sophisticated practical joke when, after minutes of waiting to proceed along what appears to be a quiet village street and with not another vehicle in sight, you are eventually reassured by a small convoy heading your way, shortly after which you are allowed to proceed.

From the south, the turn-off is to the right and about 500m on from the first Gouvia signpost. A further right turn into a narrow dirt road that follows the water's edge to a dead end takes you to a photogenic spot where, along a narrow promontory, a tiny church sits on a small circle of land only marginally larger than the base of the church. The yachts moored nearby and an almost completely submerged caique framed by the lush green of the cyprus trees on the adjacent coastline paint a scene that rivals Pontikonissi. The lack of freshly whitewashed walls and the dilapidation of the derelict caique make a much more natural picture, a poor man's mouse island that gets my vote.

Gouvia Marina

A project of the NTOG and one of many (approximately 12) around Greece, the aim is to provide better quality marinas and more of them.

The enthusiasm for the project shown by its director and those involved in making the plans a reality is impressive. It is a shame that the venture may lose some of its good name because the facilities are not yet completed: berths are in use and therefore come under critisism from those who see a full scale marina with incomplete and inadequate facilities.

Already available is a fresh water supply at each berth and an "address system" for locating vessels, metered telephones and a limited number of showers. Yet to be installed are power and telephone links to each berth, a club house, bank, OTE, post office, tennis, basketball and volleyball courts plus customs immigration and port police offices. At the moment, all vessels entering Greece via Corfu must first report to the authorities in the new port area at Kerkyra before proceeding on to the marina.

Unfortunately the work in progress has left large holes in the embankment and this is potentially dangerous at night. Started some fifteen years ago, the work is expected to be completed in

1994. I am informed by the management that charges are a tenth of those in Italian marinas; perhaps a token price of 578drs per day for a 10ft vessel will help those who know about such things to make a comparison.

Weather forecasts for the Ionian region are posted on the office door.

Kondokali

Except for the ambiguous "Attention Pedestrians" sign, you might pass by on the main road to Kerkyra from Paleakastritsa and never know that the resort of Kondokali was there behind the buildings and trees. The beaches here are very small and infrequent, in coves amongst the trees and the scene is more like that of a lakeside complete with forested islet (Lazaretto or Gouvino) off shore. Nearer the capital neglected and rusty ships from bygone ages are moored.

Potamos

This large village is best approached from the north as, from the centre of Kerkyra, having bounced your way over the pot holes on the road from San Rocco square, you pass all the junk yards, grubby businesses and typical roadside buildings until you come to a fork in the road. A signpost is strategically placed to let you glimpse the name of the village along the turn-off that you have just sailed past. What you have just over shot is Potamos.

Within the village the new houses are on a grand scale but in the old village the buildings, tatty as they may be, have more appeal. As the name indicates, the settlement is on a river where a sign on the bank advises us to look after it, as rivers bring life.

SEVENTEEN

Accommodation in Corfu

The National Tourist Organisation office in Kerkyra annually produce a list of hotels and apartments on the island (though incomplete) and will give out copies of the appropriate section. While many people have reservations as part of a package holiday, many others arrive "on spec" and, with the mass influx of Italian tourists in August, the island soon becomes full.

Until this happens there are plenty of the usual room touts in the port arrivals hall ready to transport people to their accommodation or camping grounds. Within the airport is a courtesy telephone service with direct links to many of the higher category hotels.

Hotels, apartments etc.

The following list has been organised into resorts in the belief that it is primarily the location of the room, and secondly the category, that usually influence decisions of where to stay.

Hotel	class	tel. no.	beds	location/comment
● **Kerkyra town**				
Corfou Hilton	L	36540	515	Kanoni
Corfou Palace	L	39485	195	Dimokratias
Ariti	A	33885	312	Kanoni
Cavalieri	A	39336	91	Kapodistriou
Corfou Divani Palace	A	38996	306	Kanoni
Anthis	B	25804	86	Kefalomantouko
Arion	B	37950	199	Anemomylos
Astron	B	39505	63	Donzelot
King Alkinoos	B	39300	102	Zafiropoulou
Marina	B	32783	192	Anemomylos
Olympic	B	30532	90	Voulefton
Phoenix	B	42290	34	Garitsa
Arcadion	C	37671	95	Kapodistriou
Archondiko Apartments	C	36350	46	Garitsa
Atlantis	C	35560	112	New port
Bella Venezia	C	46500	61	Napoleon Zabeli
Bretania	C	31129	83	K. Georgaki
Calypso	C	30723	34	Vraila
Dalia	C	32341	32	Eth. Stadiou
Hermes	C	31747	62	Markora
Ionion	C	39915	144	New port
Kastro Apartments	C	34965	95	Kanoni
Royal	C	37512	232	Kanoni
Salina	C	36782	31	Alikes Potamou
Salvos	C	32001	176	Kanoni
Akropol	D	39569	37	Zavitsianou
Constantinoupolis	D	39826	94	Zavitsianou
Europa	D	39304	70	Neos Limin
Metropolis	D	31156	25	L. Konstantinou
New York	D	-	74	
Cypros	E	30032	39	Agion Pateron
Elpis	E	30289	30	N. Theotoki
Karmen	E	36341	31	Kefalomantouko
Kriti	E	38691	23	N.Theotoki
Spilia	E	25648	35	Solomou

Hotel	class	tel. no.	beds	location/comment
● Aghios Georgios				
Belle Vue	B	-	52	
Golden Sands	B	51225	87	
Ananias	C	-	46	furnished apts.
● Aghios Georgiou				
San George	D	-	30	
● Aghios Gordis				
Aghios Gordios	A	53320	388	
Alonakia	B	53102	30	
Chrysses Folies	C	53106	40	
Diethnes	D	53105	30	
Pink Paradise	E	44710	21	
Pink Paradise ll	E	44710	70	
● Aghios Ioanis (Karousades)				
Sidari beach	C	95215	55	
● Aghios Ioanis (Triklini)				
Marida Pension	A	52410	26	
Vladinmir	C	52465	40	
● Aghios Stefanos (west)				
Nafsika	C	31240	31	
Saint Stefanos	C	95284	16	
Banos Studios	D	-	18	furnished apts.
Romance	E	-	18	
● Aharavi/Anaharavi				
Century Resort	A	-	28	furnished apts.
Filorian	A	93107	40	furnished apts.
St George's Bay Club	A	93203	120	furnished apts.
Aharavi Beach	B	93146	82	
Chryssa Pension	B	-	31	
Ionian Princess	B	93110	198	
Adazio	C	93066	32	furnished apts.
Anastasia Beach	C	-	30	furnished apts.
Beach Side	C	93001	34	furnished apts.
Flora	C	93214	33	furnished apts.

Hotel	class	tel. no.	beds	location/comment
Marie	C	93106	46	
Kormorandos Beach	D	-	49	
● Alikes				
Kerkyra Golf	A	31785	444	
Alykes Beach	C	37628	39	
Salina	C	36782	31	
Sunset	C	31203	101	
Triantafylia	E	33354	19	
● Analipsis				
Dimitra	D	-	48	furnished apts.
● Ano Pavliana				
Iliovassilema	D	55149	16	
● Argirades				
San Giogio	C	51303	52	
Galazia Thalassa	E	-	20	
● Arilas				
Arilla Beach	C	51201	68	
Marina	C	51100	32	
Marvellus Arills	C	51120	29	
● Armenades				
Kourkoulos	C	-	83	
● Astrakeri				
Angela Beach	B	31279	80	
Astrakeri Beach	C	31238	75	
Sandra	E	31120	28	
● Barbati				
Alexiou	B	91383	104	
Akos Apartments	C	91276	18	furnished apts.
Barbati	C	93594	54	
Irene's Studios	C	-	12	furnished apts.
Nautilus	C	93620	114	
Nireas	C	-	38	furnished apts.

Hotel	class	tel. no.	beds	location/comment
● Benitses				
Odyssey Apartments	A	92227	112	furnished apts.
Regency	A	92305	343	
San Stefano	A	36036	470	
Achilleus	B	92425	138	
Belvedere	B	92441	342	
Eugenia	B	92064	36	
Hesperides	B	92374	32	furnished apts.
Potamaki	B	30889	320	
Bavaria	C	92592	35	
Bella Vista	C	92087	42	
Corfu Maris	C	92381	48	
Kamares Benitson	C	92270	56	
Karina	C	92385	44	
Le Mirage	C	92026	44	
Loutrovia	C	92258	44	
Mary	C	31809	14	furnished apts.
Avra	D	92424	37	
Benitsa	D	39269	28	
Agis	E	92393	40	
Eros	E	92393	40	
Riviera	E	92258	30	
● Boukari				
Boukari	C	22687	20	
Penelope	C	51483	23	
● Dafnila				
Dolianitis	E	-	28	
● Dassia				
Corfu Chandris	A	33871	558	
Dassia Chandris	A	33871	467	
Elaea Beach	A	93490	366	
Eva Palace	A	91237	323	
Grecotel Dafnila Bay	A	35836	481	
Margarona Palace	A	93742	219	
Ekaterini	B	93350	36	furnished apts.
Palma Beach	B	93040	70	
Paloma Bianca	B	93575	64	

Hotel	class	tel. no.	beds	location/comment
Sofia Pension	B	93256	15	
Amalia	C	93520	48	
Anna	C	-	16	
Dassia	C	93224	102	
Dassia Margarita	C	93224	50	
Galini	C	91248	20	
Kar Mar	C	93484	24	furnished apts.
Keti	C	24013	18	furnished apts.
La Calma	C	-	42	
Laskaris	C	-	42	
Meropi	C	-	12	furnished apts.
Nefeli	C	-	39	
Oscar	C	93371	56	
Primavera	C	91911	59	
San Remo	C	-	52	
Telemachus	C	-	145	
Tina	C	93664	35	
Scheria	D	93233	32	
Rose Garden	D	-	45	furnished apts.

● **Doukades**

Hotel	class	tel. no.	beds	location/comment
Iliolousta	C	22274	11	furnished apts.

● **Ermones**

Hotel	class	tel. no.	beds	location/comment
Ermones Beach	A	94241	504	bungalows
Athina Ermones Golf	C	94236	39	

● **Gastouri**

Hotel	class	tel. no.	beds	location/comment
El Greco Pension	B	31893	63	
Montaniola	B	56205	93	
Argo	C	39468	28	
Binzan Inn	C	56495	120	
Gefra Kaiser	C	92190	50	
Sissy	C	56240	17	furnished apts.

● **Glyfada**

Hotel	class	tel. no.	beds	location/comment
Grand Hotel	A	94201	465	
Glyfada Beach	B	94257	66	

Hotel	class	tel. no.	beds	location/comment
● Gouvia				
Dembonos	A	33708	95	
Grecotel Corcyra Bch.	A	30770	487	
Prifitis House	A	91263	24	furnished apts.
Angela Pension	B	91336	38	
Aspa Pension	B	91165	33	
Filipas	B	91335	28	furnished apts.
Molfetta Beach	B	91915	49	
Paradissos	B	91438	76	
Park	B	91530	378	
Artemis	C	91509	53	
Constantinos	C	91431	23	
Elizabeth	C	91451	39	
Galaxias	C	91223	67	
Gouvia	C	91317	40	
Iliada	C	91360	100	
Louvre	C	91506	43	
Maltezos	C	91667	40	
Pheacion	C	91497	70	
Popi	C	91500	93	furnished apts.
Sofia Gouvia	C	40618	23	furnished apts.
Sun Flower	C	91568	23	
Theodora	C	91500	93	
Haraklia	D	91393	35	
Orfeas	D	91436	34	
Sirena	D	91458	34	
Adrias	E	91223	28	
Homeric	E	91471	29	
Mathos	E	-	14	
Omikron	E	91471	22	
Passas	E	23223	19	
● Ipsos, see also Pirgi				
Sunrise	B	93414	72	furnished apts.
Ypsos Beach	B	93232	114	
Doria	C	93582	39	
Ionian Sea	C	93241	14	
Jason	C	93583	67	
Mega	C	93208	100	

Hotel	class	tel. no.	beds	location/comment
Platanos	C	93240	58	
Costas Beach	D	93205	22	
● Kalami				
Villa Matella	A	-	18	
Kalami	C	37595	20	furnished apts.
● Karoussades				
Corfu Mirabel	B	-	145	
● Kassiopi				
Frossyni's Gardens	A	81258	38	furnished apts.
Poseidon	A	81439	16	furnished apts.
Balari	B	81220	16	furnished apts.
Jerry's Apartments	C	81317	18	furnished apts.
Martzoukos	C	-	15	furnished apts.
Mikelantzelo	C	35610	17	furnished apts.
Oasis	D	-	25	
Edem	E	81431	28	
● Kavalerina				
Sioux	C	44018	15	
● Kavos				
Roussos Pension	B	22122	15	
Saint Marina	B	61345	104	
Alexandra Beach	C	22281	46	
Cavos	C	22107	39	
Dimitris	C	-	13	
Morfeas	C	61300	84	
Pandis	C	-	20	furnished apts.
Sotiris Alaxander	C	-	16	furnished apts.
Cavo Palace Alex.	D	-	16	
Panela Beach	D	61328	40	
Mathos	E	-	14	
● Komeno				
Astir Palace Corfu	L	91490	590	
Kerkyra Club Marina	A	91504	46	furnished apts.
Radovas	A	91218	221	

Hotel	class	tel. no.	beds	location/comment
Komeno Villas	C	91953	34	furnished apts.
Sylvana	C	25611	20	furnished apts.

● Kondokali

Hotel	class	tel. no.	beds	location/comment
Kondokali Palace	L	38736	467	
Intermezzo Apartments	A	91338	18	furnished apts.
Great Alexandros	C	91239	44	
Ledra	C	91550	45	furnished apts.
Pyrros	C	91206	49	
Spiti Rengis	C	-	18	furnished apts.
Telessila	C	91821	63	
Hariklia	D	91393	34	
Panorama	D	91239	38	
Adrias	E	-	28	
Aleka	E	91291	18	
Angelos	E	91291	18	
Barba Dimos	E	91446	24	
Rozina	E	91459	33	

● Liapades

Hotel	class	tel. no.	beds	location/comment
Elly Beach	A	41455	78	bungalows
Liapades Beach	C	41294	34	
Liapades Beach ll	D	22115	57	

● Messongi

Hotel	class	tel. no.	beds	location/comment
Apollo Palace	A	55433	188	
Gemini	B	55398	75	
Maria House	C	38684	35	
Melissa Beach	C	55229	56	
Rossis	C	55352	57	
Roulis	C	55353	30	
Toxotis	C	55398	44	

● Moraitika

Hotel	class	tel. no.	beds	location/comment
Miramar Beach	L	30183	285	bungalows
Delfinia	A	30318	151	motel
Albatros	B	55315	101	
Alkyonis	B	55201	110	
Capodistrias	B	55319	53	bungalows

Hotel	class	tel. no.	beds	location/comment
Delfinakia	B	55450	71	
Delfinakia ll	B	55450	82	
Messonghi Beach	B	38684	1587	
Solonaki Pension	B	-	33	
Bella Grecia	C	-	94	
Margarita	C	55267	67	
Prassino Nissi	C	55379	50	
Sea Bird	C	55400	31	
Three Stars	C	92457	58	
Fondana	D	55281	26	
Pirgolambida	D	-	32	
Moraitika	E	55345	32	

● **Nissaki**

Nissaki Beach	A	91232	443	
Asprochori	C	91266	72	furnished apts.

● **Pagi**

Magdalini Apartments	C	-	12	furnished apts.

● **Paleokastritsa**

Akrotiri Beach	A	41275	238	
Oceanis	B	41229	123	
Paleokastritsa	B	41207	293	
Pavillon Xenia	B	41208	14	
Apollon	C	41211	46	
Eftichia	C	-	12	furnished apts.
Lyssippos	C	-	15	furnished apts.
Odysseus	C	41209	64	
Hermes	D	41211	38	
Zephyros	D	41244	34	
Bourbos	E	41209	28	
Fivos	E	92424	21	
Paleo Inn	E	41220	40	

● **Perama**

Alexandros	A	36855	163	
Aeolos Beach	B	33132	673	bungalows
Akti	B	39445	107	motel
Oasis	B	38190	124	

Hotel	class	tel. no.	beds	location/comment
Aegli	C	39812	71	
Continental	C	33113	40	
Faliraki	C	92121	31	furnished apts.
Fryni	C	36877	34	
Pontikonissi	C	36871	84	
Bretanos	D	92350	15	furnished apts.
Annita	E	33146	32	
Perama	E	33167	31	

● **Perithia**

Saint Spyridon Bay	B	-	76	bungalows

● **Pirgi** see also Ipsos

Anna Liza	A	93438	72	furnished apts.
Omonia	C	93417	21	furnished apts.
Pyrgi	C	93209	106	
The Port	C	93293	14	
Ionia	D	93349	36	
Mina	D	93404	34	furnished apts.
Palmira	D	-	16	furnished apts.
Theo	D	-	39	
Villa Katerina	D	932969	9	furnished apts.

● **Platonas**

Platonas	D	31396	44	

● **Potamos**

Elvira Pension	B	91995	76	
Gefiraki	C	30059	52	
Zorbas	D	37654	31	
Spyros	E	32979	29	

● **Rigglades**

	C	23084	16	furnished apts.
Maria	C	23084	16	furnished apts.

● **Roda**

Roda Studios	A	-	16	furnished apts.
Coral	B	-	28	
Roda Beach	B	93202	685	
Aphroditi	C	93147	40	

Hotel	class	tel. no.	beds	location/comment
Milton	C	93295	46	
Roda Oasis	C	-	41	
Semeli	C	-	56	
Silver Beach	C	93134	63	
Village Roda Inn	C	93358	32	
Ninos	E	93291	32	
● Sidari				
Afroditi Beach	C	95247	35	
Aleca	C	33635	8	furnished apts.
Astoria	C	31315	36	
Mimoza	C	95363	67	
Selas	C	95285	41	
Sidari Alcyon	C	-	68	
Three Brothers	C	31242	70	
Sidari	D	95226	16	
Sidari Star	E	95276	19	
● Sinarades				
Yaliskari Palace	A	31400	420	
● Triklino				
Nora	D	-	32	
Ideal	E	52282	26	
● Tzavros				
Ionian Arches	B	91650	20	furnished apts.
● Vatos				
Vicky	E	94318	12	

Camping

Corfu has at least one camping ground at all the resorts, many have hut type accommodation and all have tents that may be hired. Prices are standard at 500drs per person per day plus extra for a variety of facilities such as washing machines and irons etc.

Hostels

Despite what the NTOG lists show, there are surprisingly no Youth Hostel Association premises on Corfu. One camping ground at Kondokali apparently has hostel type accommodation but when I enquired at the reception desk, the owner screamed at me that he didn't want anyone to stay there, he wanted to be alone. They were filling the swimming pool the next day so perhaps he has had a change of heart.

EIGHTEEN

Food and eating places

Local specialities

The dishes here described as local specialities are native to Corfu and very seldom found in restaurants elsewhere. Below I have given some details of these dishes as they were given to me by a cook, with the aim of trying to help you decide if you want to order them. But more detailed recipes are included in the books on sale in a variety of languages in most souvenir shops.

Burdetto
A small portion of fish (the type isn't listed in *Fishes of Greece* so I can't give its English or Latin name), or very rarely eel (they would warn you) covered in a slightly oily red sauce that is extremely tasty and rather tangy and needs either spaghetti or fried potatoes to soften the strong flavour. Half fry the fillet of fish in a sauce of red and black pepper, then add water, oil, lemon juice, tomato paste and sugar to taste.

Sofrito
Stroganoff-like lengths of meat in a white sauce that is delicious with rice. Fry the tenderised beef (often advertised as veal) slices, floured, and flavour with garlic and parsley. When half cooked, add cup of vinegar water and thickening.

Pastitsada
Not to be confused with Pastitsio (macaroni pie): chunks of beef braised in a highly spiced red sauce and served on top of channel tunnel size macaroni. I didn't personally like it because the macaroni was usually under cooked and cold. It will occasionally be made with cockerel in place of beef and will then be considered a delicacy.

The best of both worlds

In searching out traditional restaurants in Kerkyra to recommend, I had become rather self congratulatory, as they aren't easy to find and I had located a fair few. I was brought sharply back to earth one evening when I made a return visit to what had struck me as a tiny family taverna with a good selection of dishes. There were just seven tables outside, only four of which were occupied, and possibly one or two around the corner of the little kitchen. However, they completely muddled my order and from then on I paid attention. I could hear waiters calling orders for food that never seemed to appear and it was hard to believe that the people at the other three tables had ordered so much. Then another party arrived and because the table was too small, were ushered into the kitchen. So I made a point of going into the kitchen myself before I left, and I had to laugh and admire their ingenuity in having a "family taverna" at one end of the kitchen and a thirty table fast food restaurant at the other!

Dionisos, 17 Dona Street. Behind the Acropol Hotel in the old port square.

Eating places in Kerkyra

O Sotiris 2 Perouladon Street. The name of this *psistara* (roast meat taverna) is masculine but the cook, who is an expert, is female as are all the staff within this family run establishment. On most evenings they have a lamb or pig spit roasted to perfect tenderness plus stuffed pork roll and chicken. Though the meat is cooked to perfection the service and *tsatsiki* are appalling.

Take the coast road out of Kerkyra towards Gouvia and take the middle of the three lanes until a break in the kerb allows you to turn left (inland!) in front of a huge area of waste ground. Continue straight and between the buildings there until you come to a T-junction, turn left into the one way street and the taverna is 20m along on the left. It would be unlikely to cost more than the minimum taxi fare from the centre of Kerkyra.

O Yannis Anemomylos. They had some unusual dishes here including spicy fat sausages in a tomato sauce that were delicious and ridiculously inexpensive. Their He ma (local wine) was very good and only 170drs a half litre.

Take the road towards Kanoni. Just past the Douglas Obelisk where the road curves right and up to Analipsis you need to go down the street with the no entry sign (preferably on foot!), and after 100m and opposite number 56 is the taverna, on the right through a little gate. Go early because it is very popular with the locals and every one else who has ever eaten there.

Mezedakis 38 Ethnikis Antistasis Street. To quote from their menu: "We have started the Mezedakis in an effort to bridge over the present with the past, rediscovering long lost tastes, a company for drinking your wine. As the ancients said 'The best meze for the wine is the company you are drinking with,' we contribute the meze, you add the company and lets see what happens." Mezé (both e's are soft) are the titbits that are served with ouzo and wine to enhance the flavour and enjoyment of the drink. The enterprising owner here has gathered together a mind-boggling selection of traditional mezé and has brought ingredients from all over the country to assemble rare delights such as the rock hard, highly spiced sausages from Ioannina, camel pie, fried mussels, braised testes and roast tongue. Don't be put off by these items if you are of a squeamish disposition, there are plenty of non controversial dishes such as fried cheese, stuffed peppers, cheese balls and the more common tsatsiki, taramosalata, garlic sauce and potato salad etc. A selection of the best of Greek wines is available plus imported brands and the atmosphere is very convivial despite a mosquito problem. Middle to high price range but worth the experience.

Take the coast road out of Kerkyra heading north and after four and a half kilometres a group of buildings including several restaurants and discotheques is seen on the left hand side of the road. Mezedakis is in the middle of the cluster and visible from the road.

O Bekios Ethnikis Antistasis Street. The better of two *psistaras* in the row of shops just before the T-junction described in the directions for "O Sotiris", above.

O Vlahos (the peasant/fool!) 5 Xenofondos Stratigou Street. With room for only four tables inside and not many more outside, the numbers are kept to a level that the frail looking little old lady can cope with serving. Her husband prepares roast lamb, kokoretsi (a crunchy spit roasted pork dish that includes liver), chicken and stuffed pork roll from his unique recipe that he found during his days as a sailor. You may be unlucky and find them sold out of the latter, as many ships send someone to buy up all the *rolló* when they dock.

Opposite the new port buildings on the corner of the second turning to the left going away from town.

The Red Dragon Opposite the Mon Repos gates, Analipsis. You may be forgiven for mistakingly thinking this restaurant is called To Steki Mas (our haunt) as these are the most noticeable signs which cover a whole wall. They have an astonishing selection of dishes including all local specialities which aren't always translated onto the English section of the menu. If you want to try something unusual like the excellent *bourdétto,* ask for their advice.

O Nikolouzos 20 Solomou Street. A good selection of dishes and inexpensive. Good "heady" Hée ma.

Ten metres downhill from the bus station near the New Fort.

O Spiros 16 Guilford Street. Worthy of a mention because of their Tas kebab, a spicy beef dish. 100m uphill from the town hall square and on a right hand corner.

Averof 4 Prosaledou and Alipiou. Not to be confused with the fast food restaurant of the same name. From the Ionian Bank in the square at the side of Aghios Spiridonas, with your back to the church, turn right and it is 20m down on the left.

Orestes 78 Xenofondos Stratigou. Pleasant garden setting with a good reputation but I found the food disappointing, and they agreed that the spinach pie I had ordered was stale. Signposted from the coast road towards Gouvia and set in the one way street 100m nearer town than "O Sotiris" (see above).

Some places which disappointed were the **Skouna** in the square in front of the Mitropolis Cathedral, where the stifado was so vinegary that I had trouble eating it; **Vlahi,** in a basement near the New Fort bus station, which had wonderful country chicken but a very off putting stench of tom cat; **O Faros,** with tables under the trees skirting Garitsa Bay, which was a nightmare of mosquitos and had terrible food, right down to the salad.

For those who want a break from Greek cuisine there are three Chinese restaurants: **The Mandarin Palace** near Gouvia, **The Courser** at Ipsos, and **The Lotus Garden** at Ano Messongi. British-run fish and chips shops are found at Benitses and Ipsos and the taste is just like back home!

Most resort restaurants offer familiar sounding items such as cornish pasties and steak and kidney pies, and these are supplied to outlets all over the island from **The English Oven** bakery in Kerkyra. Run by an English couple, the scrupulously clean looking premises also do a take away service of their very tasty range. The bakery is at 11 Napoleon Street and is best reached from the road that passes the new port, second turning left past the roundabout, and then follow the signs for the Hotel Europa.

NINETEEN

Nightlife

There is a wide variety of evening entertainment available on Corfu, from sitting at a quiet waterside bar enjoying the sunset over an ouzo to losing your shirt at the casino.

Greek dancing

All the resorts have at least one well advertised restaurant that puts on a display of Greek dancing, and lessons will be given to those who can't resist the temptation to join in. For those staying in quieter areas, there are the Hellastours' excursions to Tripa and Danilia where the same thing on a grander scale is organised (see page 183).

There is a completely unadulterated form of the same thing at the *bouzóuki* Corfu By Night, 5km out of Kerkyra towards Dassia, but no tuition will be given and prices are astronomical.

Cinemas

There were three cinemas in Kerkyra when I arrived and two when I left. To be more accurate there was only one open — an outdoor cinema in Marasli Street that has daily performances at 22.00hrs. The second had closed for a month to complete the seasonal convertion between an outdoor and an indoor establishment. This was at the Rex in G. Theotoki Street halfway down on the left away from San Rocco. The third was up for sale.

The only cinema outside the town is in the middle of nowhere, 4km from Danilia village away from Kerkyra, where a screen sits in a field and the sign declares it to be a drive-in-cinema, which would explain the lack of seats. No further details are given and I have heard tell that it shows pornography but can't confirm this.

Casino

The casino is at the moment in the Achillion Palace but there are rumours of a move to the Corfu Hilton hotel. Courtesy buses leave from in front of the old fort every hour. Open from 20.00 to 02.00 on weekdays and to 03.00hrs on Saturdays and Sundays. Closed at Easter and during elections. The smallest stake is 500drs and the largest 500,000drs. Admission is 1,000drs and passports and smart dress are required.

Sound and Light Show

The NTOG organise a Sound and Light show in the grounds of the Old Fort. The displays of folk dancing by professionals wearing traditional costume were very impressive, despite the distinct resemblance of the attire of the male dancers to dresses. A four-piece band accompanied them and later played some of the more well known tunes.

The top of an incredibly vulnerable looking scaffolding with wooden plank seating arranged to give a view of the sea and town to the north, is the setting for the Sound and Light display. The lights consist of red and green glows on the distant shore line and an impressive display of heat lightening that they must have had divine assistance in organising. The sound was a recording of some well known but just unidentifiable actors' voices reading the most atrocious piece of English narrative that I have ever heard! "Nausica" (or perhaps that should read "Nausia") drivelled on about Odysseus until he was taken by ship to Ithaka, at which point the Minoan Lines' "El Greco" steamed past and the whole thing was a fiasco. I willingly joined the line of people leaving half way through as there is a limit to dedication to duty! In English from Monday to Fridays. Dancing at 21.00hrs sharp and Sound and Light at 21.45hrs. Price 400drs.

Concerts

The Mayor's office organise concerts by visiting orchestras on Saturday evenings throughout the summer. Previously the venue was in the cinema in Akademias Street that recently closed. For new venue check with the information office in the new port building where a pamphlet in Greek gives the programme. Details for the coming Saturday are displayed in the middle of the little traffic island at the end of G.Theotoki Street in front of the bank.

TWENTY

What to see and do

Museums

Archaeological Museum

The collection of finds from sites all over the island is housed on the first floor of the modern, airy and well lit building that was purpose-built to rehouse the sculptures from the Temple of Artemis which had previously been exhibited in the palace.

Halfway up the staircase leading to the exhibits is an excellent map of the town area illustrating to good effect the locations where the finds were made and how the settlement was originally laid out. At the top of the stairs is a "Pithos" which, as you all know, is a burial vase whose vast diameter tapers down to a tiny base, which makes it look extremely precariously balanced.

Further on, the displays of silver coins from the fifth and sixth centuries BC and a photograph of what they looked like when first uncovered inspires dreams of finding something similar in the back garden.

The *pièce de résistance* of the exhibition is in "the Gorgon room". I had read pages of explanation about exactly what it depicts but this was a mistake as the sculpture was an anticlimax, which it wouldn't otherwise have been. It must be said that to even the most uneducated eye the huge pediment from the Temple of Artemis is impressive and brings to mind images of an Acropolis like building filled with toga clad figures worshipping strange gods. Having said that, I have an obligation to describe the story depicted for those interested in learning its secrets — to avoid the disappointment I experienced, don't read the story in the box until after you first glimpse the sculpture. The size of the sculpture at 17m by 3m was particularly ambitious for the style and development of art at that period, and it is interesting to think that it was ahead of its time (590-580BC) and may well have been controversial. The effect of the figures would have been greatly enhanced by their being dramatically overpainted.

There are inscribed pillars from burial sites and a translation has been made of the script, which tells of the death of a young wife and mother and is very moving.

All the exhibits are very well labelled enabling you to understand something of their history and purpose. There is another map showing the sites around the island. This confirmed what someone had told me about the excavations 50m uphill from where I was sitting being a port — a claim which I had dismissed as being due to an overindulgence in the local wine!

An archaeological who-done-it!

Mythology relates that the Gorgon (a monstrous woman with snakes for hair and whose glance could turn any mortal to stone) was slain by Perseus. At the moment of her decapitation she gave birth to two offspring who resembled each other not at all. One was Pegasus, a winged horse, and the other, Chrysador, was quite a personable looking young man who seems to have inherited none of his mother's bad looks or habits.

The slayer is depicted to the right of the Gorgon, who has been given wings, an exaggerated tongue and the inevitable reptilian coiffure to emphasise her hideousness. She is in the act of running towards her attacker while looking to her right. The fact that these two figures are flanked by a pair of leopanthers (yes that's right: a cross between a leopard and a panther) apparently indicates that the Gorgon represents in this case the great nature goddess.

To give more detail to the work, the corners have been filled with scenes from the war between the Olympian gods and the Titans. On the right, Zeus (the beardless young man) is attacking an enemy with a thunderbolt and on the left a similarly menacing situation exists but the identities are less certain. It might be Priam being threatened by Neoptolemos, it might be Kronos being threatened by Poseidon, or then again it might be Rhea in the vulnerable position. Everyone will make up their own minds!

The Archaeological Museum is located in Vraila at right angles to Dimokratias, the coast road, and well signposte/. You might be forgiven for mistaking the welfare office next door for the entrance so look for the pottery shards outside the door. Toilets on the ground floor. Admission 300drs, students 200drs. Open from 08.30 to 15.00, not Mondays.

The Museum of Asian art

Housed in the Palace of St Michael and St George the exhibits are largely from two private collections. In 1919, Gregorios Manos, an ambassador to Austria who had also lived in France where he was a frequent buyer at the auctions of oriental art, offered his collection of 10,000 pieces to the state with the proviso that he should receive a small pension and hold the position of curator of the Sino Japanese Museum for the rest of his life. Agreement was eventually reached and the exhibition opened in 1927, but its benefactor died in poverty a year later, his entire fortune having gone into the collection of the works of art.

The name of the museum was changed following the donation of 450 items from many eastern countries by N. Hatsivasileiou, an ambassador to India and Japan, who also served in the Greek diplomatic service in Nepal, Tibet, Siam, Korea, Taiwan and the Philippines. Two other diplomatic bequests have been added to the collection, which is said to be one of the finest of its kind even if it is the last thing you expect to find in a regency palace on a Greek island!

Open from 08.30 to 15.00hrs every day except Mondays. Admission 400drs, students 200drs. A souvenir catalogue with details of all the exhibits and many colour plates is sold in the reception, price 800drs.

The Solomos Museum

The hours posted are from 17.00 to 20.00 Monday to Friday. When they do open and the wind doesn't blow the door shut, there is a grey haired professor type and a young lass with glasses (but no long hair to let down) within, who will take your 50drs admission fee for the private company that sponsors the building.

For the visitor with no knowledge of Greek literature, the entrance fee is just about justified by looking at some old photographs and oil paintings of the country's national poet: Dionysios Solomos 1795-1857. For those with an interest in poetry whose Greek isn't degree level the whole experience is frustrating, as there are so few items in English: only the first page of a biography that gets as far as his tenth birthday before leaving you considering breaking into the cabinet to read successive pages; and an article in the *Hellenic Times* commenting on how little known is the poet outside his home land; and a most peculiar document that claims to contain copies of the original court transcripts that proved the poet not guilty of raping a fifteen year old servant girl.

When I asked to see a translation of his poems, perhaps just the words of the National Anthem, they told me that the works hadn't been translated. I pointed to the bibliography at the end of the Hellenic Times article that gives a fairly long list of translations, and they then rummaged around and gave me a book to read that had been sent to them by the author: an English professor at Oxford. The book was very heavy analysis of the poet's style and all quotes were in Greek except for a solitary passage of four lines, and I am certainly not going to offer these for an opinion.

The museum is located in the house in which the poet lived after moving to Corfu from his home in Zakynthos at the age of 33. The house has been rebuilt after being damaged in the war and is located at 4 Arseniou, just past the Corfu Sun Motors office and up a short flight of steps and on the left.

As perhaps with many poets, Solomos had an emotionally disturbed and dramatic life. Even his parentage was controversial as his father was an Italian speaking count and his mother a Zantian maid servant in the former's mansion. They were married the day before his father's death when the poet was nine years old and just before he was sent under the care of a priest to study in Italy, as was the custom of the day.

The biographies don't mention the rape case that occurred when he was just 16 and involved a fifteen year old girl who fell pregnant. She was a servant who had worked for seven years in a local house and the defence spent no little time besmirching her character. It seems strange to find a thirty page booklet on this one specific episode in his life as one of the only English publications there.

A younger step-brother tried to disinherit Dionysios and his natural brother, and during the defence he was forced to denounce the mother to whom he had once been so close and whose rejection must have wounded him so much. This troubled time seems to have inspired his work rather than repressed. Although he had studied in Italian, French and English, his decision to write the majority of his poems in Greek was revolutionary. At last the Greek people had a poet that the average person could understand, and this marked the beginning of a new culture.

The Paper Money Museum

I was given various involved directions for finding the branch of the
Ionion Bank of Greece whose first and second floors house this
exhibition. The simplest way is to go to Aghios Spiridonas church
and in the small square on the side furthest from the spire is the
bank; go through the doorway nearest the church. The collection
can be seen from 09.00 to 13.00 Monday to Saturday.

Don't be discouraged if the doors are locked, the caretaker may
have popped to the loo. If it hasn't opened again after a little while,
ask the manager (the gentleman with the largest desk in the middle
of the floor on the public's side of the counter) in the banking hall
next door.

The first floor rooms contain a display of the earliest bank notes,
cheques, loan certificates, bonds, stamps and bank ledgers all of
which are very well displayed and labelled. The empty pockets
aren't due to light fingered visitors taking home souvenirs, but are
set in place for the day when the directors hope to be able to
purchase exhibits to complete the collection.

Even more entertaining is the second floor display which details
the complete process of bank note production both of old and with
the latest technology. From the original artist's sketches to the end
quality control and packaging, the stages are explained with the aid
of models, photographs and texts in both Greek and English.
Enlargements are shown of some famous fakes alongside the
originals, and the craftsmanship involved in the engraving can be
fully appreciated. Free admission.

Sinarades Folkloric Museum

The museum that I spent the most time seeing round is the tiny two
storey museum that has been made from two traditional village
houses.

Going into Sinarades, there is a tiny signpost pointing up a
narrow concrete turning directly opposite the bell tower. Up this
lane, the road divides with no clue as to where to go. Take the left
fork and continue up until you reach a telegraph pole on a corner
to the right and then look for someone to open the door for you.
The sign on the door says that the museum is open from 10.00 to
14.00 every Sunday for an admission charge of 125drs, but it may
be open on Saturdays and closed on Sundays. This isn't a problem
as if you find someone sitting in a nearby doorway (not during siesta
time), smile and say "moo sée oh" and make key turning mimes
and they will probably go and find the caretaker or someone else

Theodora Lindodoy holding the oversized key to the folklore museum at Sinarades in her workworn fingers.

authorised to get the key from its hiding place. From then on communication is a problem. If you are a small group, you will be given a guided tour which must essentially make use of the few signs in English and German plus mimes from your guide.

Living history — bless her heart

Being lucky enough to understand the short cuddly black robed figure of Theodora Lindodoy, I got the benefit of all the information she had to pass on. She would pick up an exhibit and describe its use and then in desperation begin to mime it before she realised that I had answered her that, yes, I understood her. So she would pat me and thank goodness that I speak Greek and pad on to the next item muttering "Heaven be blessed she understands me!". Both floors of the Folkloric Museum are at the top of a flight of well worn steps and I felt guilty at being the cause of all the puffing and panting that was Theodora coming up the steps behind me!

Inside the museum is an old-fashioned kitchen and I was given a demonstration of which utensils were used for which dishes and the lengths people went to to get the food as close as possible to the wood of the fire in order to economise on fuel. In those days lighting wasn't by candles but wicks soaked in olive oil protruding from the corners of small metal dishes hung from a nail on the wall.

The majority of the implements there are for use in bread making. Maize flour was used and the water had to be very hot in order for the dough to rise. Unfortunately there isn't an oven on show but they can still be seen in many rural houses and are still used. The small opening is covered by a pretty tea towel and so it is possible not to notice them in the corner of a kitchen. The oven is loaded with brushwood and sticks which burn until the bricks that are its lining become red hot. The cinders are then raked out and the loaves placed carefully inside with the long wooden spoon shaped implement. Then the doorway is covered until they are baked. Village bread is usually hard when fresh but it doesn't become much harder when stale. It has a baking soda taste and to my liking it needs more salt to help it down. Baking may be a popular chore in winter but with the many loads of wood that must be carried and the heat generated by the oven, it is an exhausting labour in the summer months. Even with the cooking fire burning the light was very dim and it makes you appreciate why people's routine was organised around the hours of daylight. It is even harder to comprehend where the women found the hours to make the fantastically intricate lace work seen in the bedroom linen and even on the underwear.

Some of the more notable exhibits include a birthing stool and Theodora is happy to play the role of midwife while demonstrating its use. The new born baby was then placed in the wooden receptacle by the side of the bed until the mother returned to the fields, at which time the trough-like cradle was carried on her head. You wonder at how such a precious bundle could be safely balanced until you look at another of the exhibits, which looks like a barrel with the top cut off and half the verticle slats missing. The seven month old baby was placed inside and in it he learned not only to stand but to stand straight, as the girdle at the top was at the height of his head and he had to stand straight in order not to have the edge against him.

The Byzantine Art Museum

Closed for "works" during my visit, the museum of Byzantine art is housed in the church of the Panayia Antivouniontissa at the top of the flight of steps up from Pizza Petes. It contains mostly icons and frescoes from various of the island's churches. Enquire at the NTOG office (just around the corner) if it is open and for its hours.

The Kapodstria Museum

Probably Corfu's most famous son, Ioannis Kapodistrias (1776-1831), was born into a noble family and qualified as a doctor. As a fervent patriot he was actively involved in deposing the French occupation and supporting the Septinsular Republic of 1800-1807 in his capacity as Secretary of State. He accepted the post of advisor to the court of Tsar Alexander I, where he was held in high regard until his frustration at the Tsar's failure to support Greece's struggle for independence led him to resign. Then from a base in Switzerland he set about raising support for the cause. In 1827 he was elected by the National Assembly as the country's first president and served until his assassination in 1831 outside a church in Nafplion by two Cretans whose uncle he had caused to be imprisoned. He is buried behind the altar of the Platitera Convent in Kerkyra.

This two-room museum at what was once his family's estate is found on the road between Potamos and Evropoulis. In the centre of Potamos, where you are suddenly presented with three roads to choose from, go straight as if to ascend the steps and the road veers right at the last minute and left again further on. Continue for two and a half kilometres, take the next two left turns and then the road to Evropoulis, where you meet a split in the road and one of the two gateposts ahead holds a brass plaque. Through the gate the right hand path leads up to a pink house and to the right is the museum.

An atmosperic collection of the great statesman's furniture, paintings, books, porcelain and medals comprise the collection. Most notable to my eye were the little cabinet of unidentified ornaments and a wonderfully ornate wood burning stove. There are also thirteen acres of grounds bequeathed to the trust by the family of whom two elderly female members survive.

Open from 11.00 to 13.00 Wednesdays and Saturdays. No photographs are allowed.

Benitses Shell Museum

This museum represents something that for most of us remains as only a dream and we never find the initiative, opportunity or good fortune to turn it into reality. Here a man has lovingly collected that which fascinated him and has now displayed it to its best advantage, and it has become his livelihood.

The man is Napoleon Sagias and his fascination is with shells. He began his collection eighteen years ago quite by chance in the way great passions are born. While working as a crew member aboard one of Onassis' many tankers and during shore leave in Australia, he passed some lazy afternoons fishing off the Great Barrier Reef. In the same area was an old gentleman who could be seen gently raking the surface of the coral and sandy areas until the tide rose and ended both their recreations. They established a nodding acquaintance after a few days, until the older man approached the other to ask frantically why he had just broken a shell. Napeoleon replied that he had just run out of bait and had broken the shell to extract the meat. The older man then confided that he had been searching for many days for just such a shell and now the only specimen had been broken. Napoleon told him he had in fact broken many, at which the old man became almost hysterical, until he was shown many whole shells amongst the coral that being camouflaged by seaweed were difficult to spot.

In gratitude the collector gave him a box of shells which made an excellent start to what was to become a remarkable collection. Within a year Napoleon had become better known within the collecting circles and had a larger collection than his mentor. Both during his years as a resident of Australia and on his annual trips to tropical shores, he continues to increase his collection. Central

America is this winter's destination and his family are apparently supportive of his passion as he tells me that half of his house is taken up by exhibits that won't fit into the museum.

The exhibits are well displayed and labelled for those with a scientific interest in the subject. The collection includes some bones from the body of a whale that was washed ashore some years ago which make you appreciate just how colossal the animal must be. Sharks' jaws, stuffed and pickled snakes, scorpions and coral — in addition to thousands of shells including many valuable and deadly specimens — can be seen. Shells and, I am sorry to say, coral can be purchased as souvenirs and, for collectors, any shell can be ordered.

The visitors' book is filled with poignant messages of goodwill from the mayor and other local dignitaries, who acknowledge that such a museum is quite an achievement today, when so little is done to encourage or help would-be entreprenuers. Well worth a visit, this is quite the most enjoyable museum on the island.

Located above the Stephanos taverna 1km north of Benitses and signposted from all corners of the island! Open from 10.00 to at least 18.00hrs daily. Admission 300drs, children 200drs.

Visiting churches and monasteries

Saint Spiridon

Unmistakable owing to the red onion on top, Aghios Spiridonas is the most important Orthodox church on the island. It is located appropriately enough in St Spiridonas Street, one of the wider side streets that join Kapodistriou at right angles. Built in 1596, it replaced an earlier church of the same name in San Rocco Square that was demolished in the construction of the city walls.

Modern technology has made inroads even into religion as, if you listen carefully, you can hear an extractor fan working in the alcove around the relics to draw out the smoke from the many candles that have been lit there!

Aghios Spiridonas, the island's patron saint, is held in extremely high regard by the people, who see him as having protected the island many times in the course of its history, having saved them from both defeat by attacking invaders and from plague. To commemorate these occasions, on Palm Sunday, first Sunday in November, 11 August, and Orthodox Holy Saturday, the heavy silver reliquary is carried through the streets in splendid procession,

The traffic is stopped to allow the passage of the annual parade to the Catholic Cathedral in the square behind the town hall.

accompanied by the philharmonia and various marching bands, preceded by the Archbishop and his incense waving attendants.

The saint is much more esteemed after his demise than during his lifetime, it seems, as his only claim to fame was to have been a Cypriot bishop who attended the first Ecumenical Council of Nicaea in 325. His earthly remains were transported to Corfu by an enterprising priest, together with those of the less miraculous St Theodora, in order that they remained in Christian hands when Constantinople fell to the Turks. The sons of the priest and their descendents had possession of the Holy relics until they were "nationalised" in 1927.

Metropoli or Panayia Spiliotissa (Our Lady of the Caves)

Looking appropriately splendid at the top of a wide stairway in the little square just a few paces in from the old port is the Orthodox Cathedral that dates from 1577. Its many visitors include both Greeks and foreigners, who are always moved by the atmosphere within whether or not they are of the persuasion.

Two huge paintings on the side walls may once have been impressive icons but have deteriorated to a brown sheen and look rather like fly paper on a grand scale. To the right of the iconostasis

*You can listen to the chanting of the priests while eating
breakfast at the café in the square in front of the Metropoli.*

is an alcove outside which is an opened booklet on a lectern which informs you in five languages: "These are the remains of saint Theodora, she was a Byzantine empress, the wife of the Byzantine emperor Theophilos (829-842). (On) The first Sunday of Lent in 843 Theodora held a bishops synod in Constantinople and reinstituted the reinstatement of icons. This event is celebrated under the name of the Sunday of Orthodoxy. The relics of St Theodora were kept in Constantinople until the fall of the city into the hands of the Turks in 1453 AD. The relics were brought to Corfu together with the relics of St Spiridon in 1456 and in this way were not destroyed by the Turks."

While I was trying to scribble this down, the priest kept calling me into the alcove, even though I said I wanted to read the history first. Before I had finished, a Greek family entered and the priest began to sing the liturgy, pausing to ask the names of those to be blessed, which he popped in at the appropriate place. Then a five hundred drachma note was slipped into his pocket and the family went on their way secure in the knowledge that St Theodora would bless them and theirs.

When I entered the alcove the priest merrily began singing again until I stopped him and with thanks told him that I wasn't of the Orthodox faith. He then asked what denomination I was (perhaps having an approved version ready). When I said I am a non-believer, the lid of the reliquary was shut so quickly that poor Theodora must have felt a jolt. He wished me good health and then disappeared at top speed as if not wishing to become contaminated. I did manage to get a look at some wizened leathery grey looking hands clasped on top of richly embroidered cloth.

The mornings are the best time to join the stream of worshippers and the evenings for services.

Monastery of Panayia tou Dassou

The monastery is not easy to find from Kavos and the task may be further complicated by some of the directions you are likely to be given. At the far east end of the resort, follow the first signpost to Sweet Dreams Beach (would you believe!), at the next fork take the branch away from this beach and to the right past a house with a stepped roof, next left and up past the stables and on to the ruins at the top 1.3km away along a reasonable dirt road. At the end is a totally uninspiring and somewhat sacrilegious ruin. The church must have been recently abandoned and the decor has only just begun to be destroyed and vandalised. From one or two breaks in the undergrowth you realise how close you are to the cliff edge. You can just about get a glimpse of the white cliffs that plummet down to the sea's edge or tiny beach.

Analipsis

I was fortunate to participate in a Panayiri here on 24 May: the local celebration of the saint's day of the church from which the village takes its name. I had to park my bike at the bottom of the hill with all the other vehicles and make the ascent on foot. There were so many people going up and coming down the hill that it seemed as if all of Kerkyra had turned out for the evening. Fortunately the majority were making the return journey and not staying in the village: the area is cramped for normal purposes and now the clutter of icecream, cold drinks and popcorn stands, plastic toy salesmen, "throw the hoop" and raffle sideshows, not to mention the *souvlaki* and roasting lambs, left very little space for those wishing to stay and dance to the band that were performing on a small platform.

As the fete goers arrived at the village square, they made their way to the churchyard where someone was ringing the two bells loudly and monotonously. Everyone queued up to squeeze through the inadequate doorway to buy candles to light before proceeding on to kiss the icon and receive a piece of sweet bread before departing via the other door.

The interior of the little church bore no resemblance to its normal appearance which, like most Greek churches, is dark and gloomy. Now all the lights were turned on and aided by hundreds of candles lit by the visitors of whom women outnumbered the men by at least ten to one. Small posies of wild flowers and grasses had been gathered. Expecting to hear of a tradition or custom I asked why, and was answered "Why not!".

Pantocratoras Monastery

Everyone has vastly different accounts of the conditions of, and even the existence of, the roads up to the monastery. One guide book even goes as far as to tell you to disbelieve all the maps, there are no roads after Perithia! True that between Petalia and Lafka there is a two kilometre stretch that needs care because the tarmac surface has slipped and eroded; but it has obviously been there for some considerable time.

You can reach the monastery and mountain villages via either the turn off between the two roads to Aghios Spiridonas and hence to Loutses, Perithia and Lafka; or by way of the turning between

Sgourades and Spartilas to Strinilas (604m), where the information board informs us that the peak of Pantocratoras (904m) is 6km away. It can't be quite that far but it's hard to be exact. From the sign to where the dirt road begins is 1.4km, and on to the small parking area near the reservoir is a further 2.3km; it certainly didn't feel like more than another kilometre on foot before I reached the monastery despite the gradient.

High altitude provisions

At Strinilas, before making the ascent of the island's highest mountain, I decided to treat myself to lunch and stopped off at the Elm Trees taverna, where the food was excellent and very hot, which was my main concern as I was frozen. It is the effect of the altitude, but don't get the impression that I was experiencing any oxygen deprivation — a cigar that the idiot in the car in front of me threw out of the window was smouldering away with no problem at all!

The taverna owners, Polykronis and his Dutch wife Pauline, keep open for business every day of the year and it is a wonder they find time to make the delicious rosé wine for which they are locally renowned. They usually produce a white wine as well but the dry winter and hailstorms of the spring ruined the grapes. Fortified thus I set off for the peak, and either the powers that be have recently put in a lot of work on the roads up there or I am one of the few people who actually went there before describing it!

From Strinilas, 1.4km after the village square the tarmac gives way to a wide dirt track with the occasional bump in it to keep you awake. Another 2.3km brings you to a water storage tank. I chose to park the bike here near some other vehicles but, as it turned out there was absolutely no need for me to have abandoned my transport as even after heavy rains the route was passable all the way for cars and rider-only bikes. Bikes with a passenger would have to be of the cross country type of bike otherwise the passenger would have to get off and walk at the place where the gradient is hindered by large loose stones and gulleys, at the switch back just after the little chapel and outbuildings.

Further up, the iron rods used in the road surfacing have become exposed and left their tether to rise vertically and look most peculiar. When you near the top, a kilometre on from the reservoir, you might think you hear a squadron of low flying aircraft approaching, but look down rather than up as the noise is coming from bees flying in endless circles an inch above the surface of the

Father Evdokimos, who leads a solitary existence at the monastery on the top of Pantocratoras, Corfu's highest mountain. The antenna visible in the background is tiny in comparison with the one that straddles the courtyard of the grounds.

road, and for no discernible reason.

The ugly mould-green concrete structure of the television relay station issues sounds of the local radio station and the laughter of their visitors, which seems incongruous in such a setting. I hadn't expected technology to completely spoil the atmosphere of the monastery setting but the feet of the colossal antenna are literally in the courtyard and less than ten metres away from the little church of Christ the Saviour of all the World: Pantocratoras. Inside the chapel are two icons, one of which was on full view and in good condition while the other was almost completely covered in silver.

The scenery here is spectacular. Luckily for me, the mist which seems to permanently cover the island had cleared for half a day and visibility was at its best. This aspect of the mountain and talking to Father Evdokimos made my visit worthwhile, but the monastery buildings are certainly uninspiring even without the huge antenna straddling them.

This local man had been living at the same monastery for 47 years, 43 of which he has spent entirely alone since the death of a second monk of a stroke at the age of 53. The living quarters are cold and in the winter it is impossible for him to stay as the winds are so strong that there is a real danger of his being blown over the edge. His winter quarters are in equally unattractive iron roofed buildings just down the mountain a short way. Father Evdokimos's expression doesn't prompt attempts at conversation and he knows no other language than Greek, being rather shy. Journeys down to Strinilas, where he leads the local service, are his only break in the solitude of his existence, as few Greeks visit the site except between 1 and 6 August when the name day celebrations take place. The site was intended to be a church not a monastery.

No one else wants to share this life style and, although there are ten or more monks in the monastery in Kerkyra, he remains the only one leading such an austere life. This seems sad, although when I expressed this opinion in Kerkyra they laughed and told me it was more likely that there was what amounted to a priestly hareem in the village below. I was suprised to find the local people so cynical of a religion about which they otherwise show great enthusiasm.

Paleokastritsa Monastery

Having about the same amount of religious atmosphere as the average supermarket, this white modern looking building is in an attractive setting amongst the green of surrounding woodland, on the rocky promontory past the twin bays whose irresistible blues and greens of the sea have led it to be described as the most beautiful area of coast in Europe.

While coaches are forced to park 500m further down the hill, other vehicles can continue as far as the shaded parking area that is found between a café (whose toilets take the prize as being the worst on the island) and the entrance to the grounds. You are advised in no fewer than four languages that this is a holy place, and that proper dress must be worn. Between 1 April and the end of October the monastery is open to the public. An old woman just inside the gate holds out shapeless skirts and shawls to those in shorts and bikini tops and she will open her hand to reveal a twenty drachma piece when you hand back the clothes before leaving. It was very kind of her but I couldn't take it!

Inside you pass under a beamed tunnel where an open doorway reveals an old press that was used to make a wine that achieved some local fame. Up the steps is a courtyard that probably wasn't purpose built for the guides to assemble their flocks and give the historical details, before they disperse first to the little museum with a souvenir shop in the entrance. Priestly robes, old books, the visitor's book open at Jimmy Carter's entry, and the backbone of a whale are displayed within. No explanation is given as to what it is doing there but at least no one mentioned Jonah!

The guides inform their charges that it is the custom to light candles when entering a church, and this is the explanation for those great bundles of spindly candles in the room with the press. A small charge is made, of course, and a wizened white-bearded, black-robed monk sits inside the door and performs the religious production line of taking money and giving the candles with an expression reminiscent of the girl in the cinema foyer. The little torches are gathered up at regular intervals and recycled. I wonder if the original prayer counts after the remelt.

The histories of the various icons are explained before the queue starts for the chance to photograph the iconostasis without another fifty visitors in front of it; but don't take too long, the next coach load are already waiting in the courtyard.

Unfortunately the grounds of the monastery don't give the benefit of the view of the bays, and the next stop is usually on up to Lakones where the area is seen to its best advantage.

Aghios Athanasios Nunnery

Just before Messaria on the road from Kerkyra to Sidari an ornate sign in Greek points to the gates of the nunnery 500m along the track. Here fourteen nuns are kept busy producing icons commissioned from all parts of the island. Apparently selection of those with artistic skills for employment he training is given, but the work produced is of remarkable quality. The bars on the windows of the workshop indicate that gold leaf is used in the decoration of both the religious scenes and the frames.

Within the grounds where others of the nuns work in the fields, a new block of cells with a self contained chapel are being built. Just inside the gate is a shop where a large selection of religious tomes and lesser icons are sold to the bus loads of Greek tourists who visit there. As for us, we are welcome if we will benefit from the visit. The sisters, who are extremely hospitable, prefer groups of people rather than individuals as this causes less disruption to their work. No one there speaks English.

Incidentally, their dog goes for anyone in trousers as he has always been used to seeing habited figures.

Sir Frederick Adam, the second High Commissioner to the islands, stands proudly in front of the palace that was built at the instigation of his predecessor. To the left of the picture is the arch through which are reached .the NTOG and tourist police offices.

Buildings

The Palace of St Michael and St George

At the northern end of the Spianada is the palace that was inspired by Sir Thomas Maitland, the first Commissioner of the Ionian islands. The palace was named for the order of which he was Grand Master, and was intended to have a threefold function:

● as a Corfu head quarters for the order that was founded in 1818 and whose members were British, Maltese and Ionians who had given service to the British Empire.

● as a residence for the British High commissioner; and

● as a seat for the Ionian Parliament and senate.

The five-year construction period was supervised by the architect Colonel (later Sir) George Whitmore, and in 1824 the building began its use. When the British withdrew from the island the state assumed ownership and from 1864 to 1913 it was the home of the royal family. After suffering some internal damage during the Second World War, the three first floor reception rooms were restored in 1954 following an appeal by the British Ambassador.

The west wing now houses the NTOG, Aliens Police and Traffic Police. The arch of St Michael sees a stream of one-way traffic pass underneath it, as it straddles the main route from the Spianada to the new harbour. The main building houses the Asian Museum of Art and the library, while in the east wing are the archives, which apparently contain some works dating back to the 14th century and archives from 1797 to 1864, although the conditions in which they are stored will probably lead to their severe deterioration.

On the second floor the senate rooms and the first floor throne room contain some noted works of art; but you must stare through the doorways and are not permitted entry. The grounds are a small, well tended area that provides a welcome retreat from the bustle of the main thoroughfares. The views of the channel to the mainland and Albanian coast are enhanced by the island of Vidos in the foreground.

The Achillion Palace

Elizabeth, Empress of Austria, is a character whose life story sounds as if it has been taken from a Mills and Boon novel. As Princess of Bavaria, she was married to her first cousin Franz Joseph, but because she was from one of the lesser branches of the royal family, she was never really accepted by either the Austrians or her in-laws.

Nicknamed "Cissy", she was dominated by her mother-in-law,

who didn't trust her in the upbringing of the children and insisted on a strict disipline. Even her favourite brother was forbidden to embrace her or show any affection. She became a controversial figure and gained a reputation as a liberal thinker, helping in a non political manner in the struggles in Hungary and spending much of her time away from the Hapsburg court in her Italian villa and Bavarian Palace.

Having first visited Corfu in 1861 at the invitation of the Lord High Commissioner, staying at Mon Repos, Elizabeth developed such an affection for the island that she was presented with a gift of land that contained a villa. This villa is described in a poem that she wrote, one of the exhibits displayed in the Achillion.

She commissioned a neoclassical temple-like building but got instead a large Pompeii style palace that is the subject of much criticism. Cissy didn't like it herself and wanted to sell it, but finally decided to keep it as she was so fond of the island; so she set about furnishing the rooms piece by piece.

Within the palace are a Delarobia wall relief from their family table in front of the harmonium, and ceiling frescos by Galapeii depicting the four seasons. The chapel icon by Mach that was given in gratitude by the people of Hungary depicts the scene where she was crowned Queen of Hungary, although the people did not wish to have Franz Joseph as King. An anonymous Hungarian artist painted the scene of the trial of Christ in the chapel where the vestments worn by the Pope on his visit are displayed. The largest work is the painting of the triumphant Achilles (which is the inspirational theme of the palace) on his chariot with the body of Hector in tow.

Further depressed by the suicide of her second son, who had been refused permission to marry a commoner, and by her husband's famous infidelities, Cissy was such a meloncholy figure that she was thought to have tuberculosis. She spent long hours in the Italian gardens which, together with the statue of the dying Achilles (with a particularly painful looking wound), are the only artistic aspects of the palace that ever receive any praise.

She was fond of the work of the poet Heine and some of his volumes and a bust are displayed in the palace together with the family diary, which was given to the purchaser of the Achillion in order that it should remain there.

In 1898 Elizabeth died as tragically as she had lived — stabbed while walking beside the lake in Geneva by the anarchist Luzzeni, who then gave himself up to the police and committed suicide.

In 1907 Kaiser Wilhelm bought the palace to use as a base for his archeological researches. Exhibits from this period include a portrait by Goche, which shows the Kaiser's deformity of having one arm longer than the other, and photographs showing him greeting visiting archeologists and supervising the unloading of the immense statue of Achilles that he brought from Berlin in 1909. The most photographed exhibit must be the saddle seat that he favoured while writing and in conferences.

The estate became a military hospital during the First World War. From 1964 it has housed a casino on the first floor, the tables of which can be seen through the balcony windows. However, it didn't measure up to my expectations of what the venue for fortunes to be won or lost should look like, largely because there is no carpeting on the floor.

On the ground floor is an information desk where two polite gentlemen are totally unable to answer enquiries about any of the exhibits, which are labelled "Please don't touch" in four languages.

The Achillion is at Gastoni, 10km from Kerkyra towards Benitses, and signposted all the way. Open from 08.00 to 18.00hrs in winter and 19.00 hrs in summer. Admission 250drs, students 150drs.

Guilford Memorial

Between the Palace of St Michael and St George and the Old Fort in Kerkyra, is the memorial to the fifth Earl of Guilford. He appears to have been either highly eccentric or potty, and must have been quite a sight for sore eyes in his attire of flowing purple robes and gold wreath headress. This famous hellenophile converted to the Orthodox religion and in 1824 re-opened the Ionian Academy that had originally been started by the French. He contributed some 25,000 books from his private library. The academy became a place for the meeting of minds and played a vital role in the education of the island's scholars, contributing to the education of some noted intellectuals of the time.

The Maitland Rotunda

Amid the greenery of the Spianada in Kerkyra is a memorial to Sir Thomas Maitland another controversial figure who was reputedly rude and often inebriated. He was the first High Commissioner, and the Palace of St Michael and St George was his inspiration.

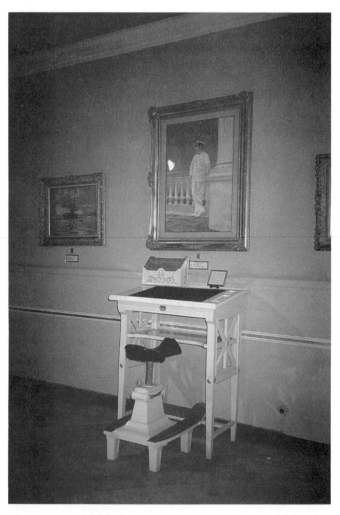

The Kaiser's saddle, which he favoured as a seat while writing and during conferences. Above is the painting of him by Goche.

In the grounds of the Achillion palace I had to politely ask the workman painting the railings if I might interrupt him for a moment and he moved begrudgingly to the edge of the picture, where his presence explains the wet paint sign.

The Tomb of Menecrates

Looking like a concrete pork pie, this tomb is in perfect condition and to those that know about such things is immensely exciting. Dating from either the sixth or seventh century BC, it is a memorial to a Corfiot consul in Oianthe on the mainland. He was drowned at sea and a grateful people erected this memorial, of which only the roof (which is not thought to be original) remains visible above the raised ground level in the unlikely location of the police station gardens.

Analipsis and Mon Repos

From the signpost to Analipsis, the road passes along the perimeter of the Mon Repos estate where the wilderness within can be seen in places where the walls are low enough.

At the top of the climb is a children's playground and a green church behind it. Directly ahead is a view down to the coast with its tapestry of blues and greens and what must be a snorkeller's paradise. Voices drifting across from an anchored yacht and the splashing of the birds were the only sounds that broke the stillness until, looking as if transported straight from Henley, two one manned rowing boats passed by, being closely pursued by a motor boat from where a coach shouted criticisms and encouragement.

Opposite the playground and set back from the road is Taverna Kardaki, to the left of which starts a stepped path leading down to the water's edge and some mini harbours. En route you pass a gentle stream of water coming from a carved lion's mouth on the rock face. It bears the inscription which is usually translated to mean that once you have sampled the water from the spring, you will at sometime return to Corfu. This is a more congenial version of the truthful translation that having imbibed you will never return to your homeland! Here many small birds dart among the darkness of the undergrowth to wallow in the pools of spring water that collect around the steps. They will chirrup angrily at your arrival.

It was this spring that became blocked in 1822 and in order to find the cause, Colonel Whitmore ordered his troops to begin digging. They found that the cut in supply was caused by a section of the altar of the previously undiscovered Temple of Kardaki having slipped where it lay buried within the grounds of Mon Repos, a stately home built for Sir Frederick Adam. Contrary to some reports, the temple ruins cannot be seen from the boundary walls. When I enquired at the gate of Mon Repos beach, I was told the story of how an intrepid photographer had chanced his arm, and probably his neck, to explore the grounds. He was lucky to lose only some skin when inspired to vault the perimeter walls, his exit assisted by two rather large German Shepherd dogs. I prefer the version that states that the temple ruins fell into the sea some years ago, especially as I don't like large dogs. The house within is now the property of the exiled Greek royal family and is where our own Prince Philip was born.

The fish farms on Lake Korission

Korission is a man-made lake — or technical lake as the Greek expression translates — made by the Venetians, who both created the channel into the southern end and strengthened it with stone walls that still look very sturdy today.

The lake is owned by the state who hold an auction every five years where the fishing rights and tenancy of the few buildings are leased to the highest bidder. The present occupiers were a syndicate of 20 men at the beginning but gradually, through lack of enthusiasm, the numbers have dwindled to just five who take it in turns to work 24-hour shifts in this lonely if beautiful setting.

The ingenious 'aquatic one-way system' at the seaward edge of the Lake Korission Fish Farms.

Because of the temporary nature of their tenancy, no one has made very much of the buildings, and there is no power, which makes the night shift difficult during their busy season when they need to be actively working 24 hours a day.

There are two "crops" of the farm: the first are the grown *Mugilidae Cephalus,* striped grey mullet, which are usually found in shallow water near the seashore or in harbours. Versatile fish, they can easily adapt to fresh water life and often enter stagnant and infected waters. Reaching up to 2kg each, the fish are packed in ice and sent to restaurants where the meat is found to be very tasty after it has been either boiled or fried.

Before their dispatch to the various outlets, the roe is first extracted then laid out on mesh to dry in the sun for a few days before being salted and waxed (sounds disgusting doesn't it!), after which it becomes ready for sale at 20,000drs per kilo! The end product should be thought of as a Greek caviar, and is not to be confused with the cod roe that is smoked before being sold as the principal ingredient for taramosalata.

Oh for a camel!

The wardens go all the way to the fish farm by bike, keeping close to the waves where the sand is firmer; but they have the incentive of 20,000drs per kilo to make it worth their while. I didn't regret having left my old bike in the dunes by the northern most edge of the lake, as it really is difficult going for all but fourwheel drive vehicles. Two people who should have known better told me that it was only a kilometre to the farm; it was two kilometres easily and over soft sand and mounds of seaweed it felt like ten! The midday sun didn't help and I began to expect Peter O'Toole to ride up on a camel at any moment. The last stretch was up the side of some sand hills, and as I plonked myself down on a bench on the bank of the channel, gesturing to the warden that I would be able to speak in a little while, the breeze from the sea seemed like a lifesaver.

Between 1 March and 1 July fishing is banned in order to allow breeding to take place unhindered. At these times you will only be able to see an example of the fish that have swum towards the fresher water flowing in from the open sea. These fish then become trapped in the arrangement of wire netting labyrinths that prevent their escape but, at the same time, allow any of the fish swimming free in the channel to enter, which they do in their own good time.

At the end of each day, the fish thus trapped are scooped out with a net and popped into the end of a large plastic pipe which scoots them back into the lake. In August, when the fish are large enough, a grade net is placed over the end to catch only those of adequate size.

The lake itself is a tranquil spot and the two kilometres long bar of sand that runs the length of it has dunes enough to accommodate those wishing to escape the crowds, although the shoreline and shallows are clogged with seaweed on the southern edge. Between Moraitika and Aghios Georgios, there are at least five turn-offs in the direction of the lake, including a signposted route opposite the road to Hlomos. None of these in fact reaches the lake and the latter leads to the northern edge of Aghios Georgios beach.

To get to the lake take either the concrete turn-off immediately to the side of the tiny petrol station at the top of the hill at Hlomotiana, or the turning right at the Mobil station where the signpost points to Aghios Mattheos. Take the way indicated to Mesavrisi. A taverna is found near the start of the dunes and in the middle of a stretch of sand is the Boring Bora, a restaurant with five rooms where the junior partner is married to an English woman. The choice of name probably reflects the character of the older gentleman there who irritated me by refusing to let the other give me a lift on his enduro bike, which would have saved me three hours walking and which delayed my very full itinerary.

Does David Bailey have this trouble?

Lake Korission with poppies in the foreground looked very splendid and deserved to be photographed. Several tracks crossing my path were obviously those left by snakes. Not having the skill to be able to tell how long ago they had passed and at what speed, I was reluctant to be standing amongst their spore without the benefit of thick trousers and socks. In my haste, I managed to have the strap in front of the lens and hence my cowardly efforts were for nothing.

The olive wood workshop

The truth of the story here is a little difficult to ascertain but it seems that we are being taken for a ride! The deception involves the use of beech wood and not olive wood for the items produced, thus cutting by an enormous amount the cost involved in producing the handmade bowls, plates and ornaments.

Beech wood is a cheaper material because it isn't naturally

grained and doesn't need drying out for four years in log form and then a further year after it has been reduced to the cylindrical lengths of the approximate size of the finished pieces. From each olive wood log, after sections that have cracks and scars have been thrown away, the usable pieces may be as little as a tenth of the original size. This is particularly true of the finest quality olive wood that comes from "cancers" in the wood where the normally straight grain becomes much more abstract. A chunk of cancerous wood one foot square by two feet in length may have taken 500 years to grow and, of course, the most desirable is the most expensive. The two lesser qualities are from the branches and stem in descending order of value. Only the innermost section of the stem is grained.

Beech wood, as previously stated, is not naturally grained and apparently the patterned effect in its products is achieved by leaving it to rot for a year, at which time the pattern appears. Then it is quickly sold before its quality begins to deteriorate. It's a bit puzzling why, when left, beech wood rots while olive wood matures! The olive wood is not varnished but rubbed with olive oil to give it the shine and rich texture.

My information comes from George Sagiadinos who served a 13-year apprenticeship. As with many craftsmen, he makes the work look incredibly easy to those who haven't actually tried to hold an implement at the right angle against a turning piece of timber on the turner's wheel. I can vouch for it being a lot harder than it looks. Even George has lost the sight of one eye as a result of an accident.

The shop, at 27 Fillelinon street in Kerkyra, which is run by George's charming wife Katerina, is open all day but should you wish to see some of the products being made, go between 10.00 to 14.00 or 17.00 to 21.00 hours and you will find George is happy to demonstrate the making of any of the items in the tiny workshop at the rear of the shop.

The Tastery

Directly opposite the gates to the Achillion Palace, an enterprising liquor manufacturer, Vasilakis A.E., whose distillery is at Aghios Ioannis, has opened a display of all their wares. You are invited to come and try as many of their extensive range as you wish.

It is your chance to try the Koum Kwat that is displayed in a huge variety of different size and shapes of bottles in many Corfu shops. I had anticipated hating this liqueur that is reputedly sweet even by

The enormous selection at The Tastery opposite the Achillion palace, where you are spoilt for choice.

standards and the intense bright orange colour is rather
... .ting.

Apparently the kumquat was introduced from Japan by a Mr
Merlin. The little fruits were consequently named after him though
they bear no resemblance to the "oranges" that completes their title.
You can see the fruit in the bottles of the liqueur but it is only
possible to taste them in the form of a "spoon sweet": preserved
fruit in a heavy syrup that is served as a dessert or to visiting guests
in Greek households, and is always accompanied by a glass of cold
water in which the spoon is placed.

Two qualities of liqueur are made; the first is the usual
fluorescent orange liquid which was every bit as ghastly as I had
suspected, but the second (called "hee mos", juice) is very pleasant
indeed and has a tangy fruity taste which I could get very fond of!
This superior recipe is also used to make mandarin, lemon,
bergamot and fruit cocktail flavours which contain no artificial
colourings and all of which were excellent.

All in all, 35 different flavours were offered plus own-brand
ouzo, vodka, gin, rum, tequila, cognac, vermouth and eleven
different wines, which are sold on the premises for 15-25 per cent
less than the retail price. Open from 09.00 to 19.00 daily.

Danilia village

There are nearly as many of the brown advertisement signs for "the
village experience" on the island as there are olive trees! On the road
to Temploni off the main Kerkyra to Paleokastritsa road, the
Danilia village is the brainchild of a local man who sadly died
recently. But his family are continuing to run this reconstruction of
a typical village as it was centuries ago, hence giving visitors the
chance to see something of the Greek way of life as it was then.

The little street is lined with workshops where you can see
craftsmen working with leather, ceramics and jewellery, plus an
abundance of souvenir shops including one run by the National
Welfare Organisation where they explain that they aim to keep the
ηditional handicrafts alive. What they don't mention is another
ירable purpose in providing a skill to orphans and girls from
־rivileged homes.

וl museum has some interesting exhibits but they aren't
־d by explanatory text as to their use or age. When the
the evening at 20.30hrs the entertainment begins and

includes traditional dancing displays, acrobatics, and a group of musicians to enjoy while you eat. Open from 11.00 to 13.00 and 18.00 until late, Monday to Saturdays.

Donkeys relaxing in the shade provided by the olives, whose knotted and gnarled trunks make them look like fairy-story trees.

Sports

Golf

The Ropa Valley golf course is managed by professional David Crawley with the assistance of Julie. Both are English and extremely friendly and helpful. The course has been internationally praised for the standard of its Pencross Bent (no, not a spinal disease you develop after too much golf, it is a famous high quality type of grass!) greens, and for Donald Harradine's design that has made full use of the river Ropa that crosses many of the holes.

The course is open from April to October, with plans to extend the season further. Those that come to play are of all nationalities and standards but of course the complete novice is not let loose. The maximum handicap is 24 for men and 36 for women. Professional tuition is available at 3,000drs per hour and clubs and trolleys at 1,300drs per day. Green fees are 5,000drs with a lot of discounts for many months of the season.

There are international tournaments from the third week of May for two weeks, the last week of September and the second week in October. Entries and all enquiries to: Mr David Crawley, Corfu Golf Club, P.O. Box 71, Corfu, Greece.

The club is open to everyone from 07.30 to 18.00. This includes the restaurant and bar that comprise the country club. To help pass the time for those members of the family who don't play golf, there are horse riding facilities (see below). In addition to the bar within the club house, there is another "Labis' 19th hole" at nearby Vatos where the minimarket, bar, snack bar and petrol station provide a 24 hour service.

Horse riding

Based at the golf club are both conventional and western riding facilities with a selection of mounts to suit all ages and standards of rider. Lessons are available if required, as are supervised rides and hard hats. Arrangements should be made by phone in advance. Tel. 94220.

Other centres that offer horse riding facilities are the Kerkyra Golf Hotel at Kondokali, tel. 31785, and a trekking facility advertised outside the first bar along the sea front road at Roda. The people behind the bar will tell you when to return to make firm arrangements, as it is difficult to track down the man who runs it.

The travel agencies in Kavos liaise with the stables there to make the necessary arrangements.

Sporting customs!

A problem for the Corfu Golf Club has been created by local customs officials who were at a loss to know what category 100 dozen golf balls came under and so what duty to charge. The figure they came up with was unacceptable and so, as happens to such items, the golf balls went for public auction. Of course, no one wanted so many; some arrangement will have to be made and the club are in a better position to find a use for them than anyone else.

The club was more fortunate when a friend arrived with supplies of 300 golfing gloves. He was stopped, and when the customs official saw 300 gloves in the suitcase, he wanted to know why they hadn't been declared. Very quick off the mark, the friend replied that he was a salesman and had brought samples of his wares, they were not for sale. To prove that they were only samples he showed that he had indeed brought only the left glove of each pair. For the uninitiated, you wear only one glove on the left hand for golf!

Tennis

All of the large hotels have an average of three courts, most of which are flood lit and open to non residents to hire. Tuition is available at the Messonghi Beach and the Ermones Beach Hotels at 4,000drs per hour.

The Corfu town tennis club has four hard courts which can be hired by non-members in the mornings from 09.00 to 13.00hrs seven days a week. You add your name to the bottom of the list and can use the court for one hour at a charge of 600drs. The courts, at 4 Romanou, are best found from the coast road past the archeological museum.

Go-Kart racing

This is available at Benitses track and at Kavos where I got stuck behind karts at midday on the main street and had to go so slowly in first gear that I was wobbling on my bike.

Watersports

What ever did we do on holiday before there was the opportunity of getting dragged around on or above the bay! The "Banana split" or "Sausage" are terms for a large phallic object that gets towed at speed behind a motor boat while people sit astride it and hang on to the handles. A variation on the same theme is the "Doughnut" which, as you might imagine, is a circular inflatable raft that you sit in rather than on. A trip around the bay costs an average of 1,000drs per person.

—**Water skiing** using both one and two skis is extensively available at 2,000 drs per session.

—**Wind surfing** is found pretty well everywhere except for the north coast beaches like Kassiopi, where the winds are too strong. 1,200drs or 2,800drs per hour with tuition.

—**Paragliding** is available at all the resorts except Kassiopi. It involves being towed by a motor boat while wearing a parachute like kite that keeps you aloft until the end of the ride. It lasts an average of ten minutes and costs 3,500drs or 6,000drs for the double version for those who want someone to witness their terror!

—**Pedaloes** aren't as popular as you might expect probably because when not in use they take up valuable space on the already packed beaches. 500-800drs per hour. More practical because they store vertically are the "canoes" which have no depression in their uniform shape so you sit on rather than in them. 300drs per hour.

—**Sailing boats** can be hired with or without tuition from Ermones beach. Price 1,500 and 3,200drs per hour.

—**Scuba diving** is officially only permitted for those with some experience and who can produce a health certificate. The diving centres can recommend local doctors for this purpose. The average cost is 5,000drs per dive. Dives may be as part of a course, as at Aghios Gordis and Ermones (where the centre is run by an English father and son team); or as part of a day trip (eg with "Waterhoppers" at Ipsos), where you will wait your turn amongst at least a dozen others for a twenty minute dive. Another centre is at Paleokastritsa, which all the clubs converge on.

Excursions

Details of the excursions and boat trips described below are available from Hellastours in Kerkyra, tel. 25053, and local travel agents.

Mainland trip

It is a shame not to see something of mainland Greece while visiting Corfu and the best way to do this is to take the excursion. You leave at 08.30 from Kerkyra. The scenery on the boat trip to Igoumenitsa is of long deserted stretches of inviting coastline. An airconditioned coach then takes you via small villages, where you can see the nests of cranes on top of telegraph poles and the birds perched precariously in them, and on over the mountains to stunning seascapes near Parga.

The Necromandeon at Ephyra is the first stop but you will already have been given a fascinating talk on the history of Greece and its people with an insight into some of the peculiarities of modern life. At the Necromandeon you can see what is one of the few sites where the priesthood practised a sinister brainwashing process on those who endured three weeks of awful preparation before being allowed in to consult the oracle of the dead. Some shameful jiggery-pokery was used to convince them that they were receiving advice from the spirits of their ancestors.

The next stop is Cassopea, or Kassopi, towards Arta where continuing excavations have uncovered the extensive remains of a complete town dating from the fourth century BC. It is possible to clearly imagine how life must have been in those times. Passing the memorial to the mothers of Zalongo, who threw themselves and their children from the cliffs to their deaths on the rocks below to escape from Ali Pasha's army, you continue on to lunch at a beachside taverna.

Nikopolis is the location of an amphitheatre which is in almost perfect condition. The guide gives many interesting facts about the history of the town that was built by Augustus Caesar in 44 BC, and has no problem making himself heard.

Even for those without any great interest in things archeological, the day is well spent. Perhaps it is not suitable for small children, as it is a long day: you arrive back in Kerkyra at 20.30. Take a snack to fill the gap until lunch and use the toilets on the ferry as the next opportunity is some hours later. The excursion costs 5,700drs.

Paleokastritsa and Sidari
You can take a trip to Paleokastritsa and the monastery, with time for swimming at Sidari. Coach trip 3,100drs.

Bouzouki night
Dinner, unlimited wine, Greek dancing display and tuition, belly dancing and plate throwing, are included in this excursion, which costs 3,900drs.

Danilia village
The trip allows time to see the village and shop before dinner and live entertainment. Cost 4,800drs

Reps cabaret
The guides put on a weekly cabaret evening and dinner. Cost 4,100drs.

Boat trips

Island hopping cruise
The vessels Petrakis and Sotirakis make twice weekly trips to Paxos and Antipaxos. You get a good look at the coast and ports of the former, and time to swim at the latter. Cost 3,650drs.

Albanian trip
This rare opportunity requires forethought, as it is necessary to give your personal details plus father's name and occupation etc. to the travel agent by the Tuesday before the departure on Saturday. The travel agent is paid 5,000drs, which includes the ferry either way and transportation to the port. On arrival you must hand over a further 8,500drs but not in drachma form. £33, $53 or the equivalent in German marks are acceptable, and either the travel agent or the National Bank will help you obtain the cash needed.

Once in Albania you are taken to two towns, Achisaranda and Eximilia, with free time at one of them. The highlight of the trip is a splendid seven course meal and entertainment of traditional music and dancing by those in national costumes. No expense is spared on the hospitality shown. The trip is subject to last minute cancellation for various reasons. Not many offices take the bookings but Ross Holidays at 11 Odos Arseniou in Kerkyra have plenty of experience.

Champagne diving
There's a weekly trip to a cave at Mourtos on the mainland where bottles of champagne have been seeded in the clear waters for you to retrieve and consume at your leisure. Cost 3,300drs.

Scuba diving
The trip includes a cruise, tuition, the dive and then lunch, and it costs 5,500drs.

The Calipso Star
This modern looking glass bottom boat makes hourly departures from Alipa Bay at Paleokastritsa and it seems that they uncover buried treasure on every trip! I can't comment personally as the vessel was moored in the middle of the bay and no one wanted to hear me hailing them. Cost 4,400drs as part of a day trip that includes the monastery at Paleokastritsa.

Coastal cruise
You can cruise from Kerkyra to Kassiopi calling at Nissaki and Kerasia. It costs 3,100drs.

Parga and Paxi
You can go swimming at Parga, with optional coach trip to the Necromandeon (see Mainland Trip), lunch on board and swimming at Paxos. Cost is 4,700drs.

Kondokali to Kouloura
Captain Spiros makes daily trips from Kondokali to Kouloura with a one hour stop at Nissaki. Depart 13.00, return 17.00hrs. Cost depends on how many want to go but about 8,000drs the boat.

Trips from Roda
Captain Kostas at Roda offers five destinations on different days: Sidari, Kassiopi, Paleokastritsa, Kerkyra and Ericoussa Island.

TWENTY ONE

Beaches

Corfu is a veritable wonderland as it has beaches of every size, shape and type to suit all tastes. They vary from those that take a good hour of difficult walking or the provision of a stout rope to reach, to those that suddenly confront you at the end of a road and then provide the challenge of picking your way over the bodies to a spot large enough to pitch your towel or sunbed; from the strips of sand stretching as far as the eye can see that usually edge shallow waters ideal for families, to the rocky bays that tempt snorkellers and divers into the mosaic of blues that the sea forms, and there to glimpse that other world below the surface of the waves; from the bays where not a ripple disturbs the surface of the crystal clear water to the beaches where the waves lift you bodily as they crash towards the shore.

Because of the incredible number of beaches and the fact that many of them have been described under the heading of the village of the same name, the information is best summarised in visual form, going clockwise from and back to Kerkyra.

Key to symbols:-
bh = boat hire, e = excursions by boat, * = sunbeds only, ** = sunbeds and pedaloes, *** = sunbeds, pedaloes and wind surfing, **** = sunbeds, pedaloes, windsurfing and skiing, ***** = sunbeds, pedaloes, windsurfing, skiing, diving and paragliding, y = yes, n = no, pc = pebbly cove, ps = pebbly strip, r = rocks, sc = sandy cove, wrs = wide red sandy beach, t = narrow sandy strip, d = difficult. The numbers in the notes column are detailed at the end of the chart.

Name of beach	Village name (if different)	Facilities	Type of beach	Food	Reached by car	More details in text	Notes
Mandouki	Kerkyra	-	r	y	n		
Garitsa	Kerkyra	-	r	n	y		
Mon Repos	Kerkyra	-	t	snks	y		1
Perama		***	t	y	to 100m	y	
Benitses		*****	t	y	y	y	
Ag. Ioannes		***	t	y	y		
Moraitika		******	t	y	y	y	
Messongi		*****	t	y	y	y	
between		-	pc	n	y	y	
Boukari		-	pc	y	y	y	
Petriti		-	pc	y	y	y	3
Notos		*	pc	y	y	y	3
Ag. Nikolaos	Petriti	-	sc	y	y		3
Molos		-	t	n	to 100m	y	4
Alikes		-	t	y	y	y	3
Bouki	Potami	-	sc	n	y		

Name of beach	Village name (if different)	Facilities	Type of beach	Food	Reached by car	More details in text	Notes
Kavos		*****	t	y	y	y	
Asprokavos	Kavos	-	r	n			
Kanula	Paleohori	-	pc r	n	to 200m	y	
Gardenios	Perivoli	*	wrs	y	y	y	
Maltas	Perivoli	*	wrs	y	y	y	
Ag. Georgios		*****	t r	y	y	y	
Korission	Hlomotiana	-	t	y	to 200m	y	3
Skidi	Ag. Mattheos	-	t r	n	n	y	
between		-	sc	n	n	y	
Prasouda	Ag. Mattheos	-	ps	n	y		
Paramona	Kato Pavl.	*	ps	y	y	y	
Ag. Gordis		*****	wrs r	y	y	y	5
Glyfada		****	t	y	y	y	6
Mirtiotissa		-	t r	snks	n	y	
Ermones		******bh e	sc r	y	y	y	

Name of beach	Village name (if different)	Facilities	Type of beach	Food	Reached by car	More details in text	Notes
Elly	Liapades	*** bh e	sc r	y	y	y	
between		-	sc	n	by sea only	y	
Paleokastritsa		****** e	sc -	y	y	y	
Ag. Georgiou	Pagi	**	wrs	y	y	y	
Arilas		**	t	y	y	y	
Ag. Stefanos W		***	t	y	y	y	3
Sidari		***	sc r	y	y	y	
Ag. Ioannes		-	t	n	100m steps	y	
Roda		***	t	y	y	y	
Anaharavi		**	t	y	y	y	
Ag. Spiridonas		*	pc	n	y	y	
between		-	pc r	n	n	y	
Imerologia	Kassiopi	**	ps	y	y	y	
Kassiopi		**	sc r	n	n	y	
Avlaki	Kassiopi	*	pc r	y	y	y	
Ag. Stefanos E		*	pc r	y	y	y	

Name of beach	Village name (if different)	Facil-ities	Type of beach	Food	Reached by car	More details in text	Notes
Kouloura		-	pc r	y	y	y	
Kalami		**	sc r	y	y	y	
Agni	Nissaki	-	pc r	y	n	y	
Kerasia	Nissaki	-	pc r	y	n	y	
Nissaki		* bh e	pc r	y	y	y	
Akti Barbati		*****bh e	t	y	y	y	
Ipsos Pirgi		****** e	t	y	y	y	
Dassia		*****	t	y	y	y	
Gouvia		***	sc	y	y		
Kondokali		***** e	sc	y	y	y	

Notes:

1 = You pay a 50drs admission fee but have the use of changing rooms and showers.
2 = The water in this area may be polluted.
3 = Seaweed problem.
4 = Access to the beach is difficult without trampling allotments. Use the entry via the new hotel.
5 = Sudden subsea shelf.
6 = Dangerous undercurrents.

TWENTY TWO

A brief history of Corfu

Historical background

Early history

Corfu and the Ionian islands have a well documented history but only from the first few centuries BC. Evidence of prehistoric settlement has been found at Gardiki dating back to 40,000BC (Paleolithic) and there is a considerable gap between these finds and those at Sidari of remains from the Neolithic period: 6000BC.

Unlike other of the Ionian Islands, Corfu is thought to have had settlers from the south of Italy and this civilisation remained undisturbed well into the Bronze Age, evidence of which was uncovered by Dorpfeld and other eminent archeologists at Afionas.

Earlier than 1000 BC there was an identified settlement known as Corcyra, sited between Garitsa Bay and the lagoon of Halkiopoulos and peopled by the Corynthians. Having grown in size and prosperity, the inhabitants severed their ties with Corynth which prompted the first documented sea battle in Greek history, in 664BC. The Corcyrans were victorious and remained independent until continuous attempts by the tyrant Cypselus of Corynth to take the island were successful.

In an internal dispute in Corynth, Periandrew had exiled his son Likofrona to Corfu until it was time for him to succeed his father. When that time arrived Likofrona, in continuing anger at his father for murdering his mother, set the condition that Periandrew take his place in exile on Corfu, which was agreed. The arrangements were thwarted by the Corfiots, who were at the time and for centuries to come bitterly divided into two political factions of Democrats and Oligarths. The Democrats killed Likofrona before he could leave Corfu, fearing that he would be sympathetic to the Oligarths.

In revenge for the assassination of his son, the tyrant Periandrew captured 300 Corfiot youths and sent them for castration, but they escaped in Samos. When the tyranny ended in 582BC Corfu was again free and prosperous enough to have its own coinage and fleet. The next attempt at occupation was in 433BC, again by the Corynthians, who were struggling to maintain control of a joint colony at Epidamnos. Athens sent ten ships to aid the Corfiots but they declined to intervene until both fleets had inflicted considerable damage on each other, at which time they sailed between them to prevent further conflict. The outcome was therefore a stalemate and this was one of the major causes of the Peloponnesian Wars between Athens and Corynth.

Corfu was engaged in its own struggles which amounted to a civil war between the two factions and this continued for many years and with many massacres until the Democrats won in 425BC. At one time Corfu promised to send 60 ships to aid Athens in the war but they never reached their destination and accounts vary as to whether they were deliberately delayed or whether storms on the journey were the cause.

Conquering armies took the island one after another and when it was occupied by the piratical Illyrians from what is now an area of Albania, an Illyrian general in dispute with his queen Teuta handed the islands over to a Roman fleet of 200 ships from Brindisi in 229BC. The islanders welcomed their new masters who allowed them pretty much self government in what was the first part of Greece to come under Roman occupation.

The Roman occupation

During their occupation from 229BC to 330AD, Corfu was an important naval base for the Romans, from which they sent ships that had been forcibly built by the islanders to defeat the Macedonians in 168BC. Once the fleet had been completed, the remaining trees were destroyed to ensure that the island was unable to build its own vessels.

In the Roman civil war, Corfu, like most of Greece, sided with Pompeii against Julius Caesar but changed allegiance, unwisely as it turned out, when the conflict was between Mark Antony and Caesar's nephew Octavian. More ships were exacted and slaves taken as crew for the Battle of Actium in 31BC after the city had been levelled by General Agripa. A period of plague hit the island and the inhabitants, who were in no fit state to offer any resistance, were given privileges for their loyalty. The Emperor Nero visited Corfu, staying at Kassiopi and worshipping at the temple of Zeus there in what was in 66AD a major town.

Accounts of Christianity being brought to the island are confused and they would have us believe that Jason and Sosipater who both studied under Paul came to the island around 200AD and, at what would have been a very great age, went on to attend the Council of Nicaea in 325AD. Certainly the first church was established at Paleopolis at what is now Anemomylos but not until Sosipater, his warder, fellow prisoners and Kerkyra the daughter of a Roman prince, had been martyred for their beliefs which were considered treasonable at the time.

At the aforementioned council was another Bishop who was to have great significance in the history of the island but not until after his death! It was, of course, St Spiridonas. The 566 years of the Roman occupation were prosperous and largely peaceful years.

Troubled times

The Byzantine period from 330AD to 1081AD saw pillaging of the islands by the Vandals in 466 and Slavic raids until the town was virtually destroyed by Totila the Ostrogoth in 562AD. In 1081 the Normans reached Corfu in their conquest of the Byzantine lands, having negotiated in advance with Venice for assistance in return for unlimited trading privileges. They went back on this agreement in favour of Pisa in 1122, in response to which the Doge personally commanded a fleet to give a demonstration of strength off Corfu.

When the Norman, Roger II of Sicily, captured the island in 1147, Venice came to the aid of the Greeks and it was liberated two years later, although there was no love lost between the allies. The Venetians refused help against a third attack, this time in 1182 and by William II of Sicily in the person of General Margaretone. When a peace was agreed in 1187, both sides were so weakened that no terms could be settled and while Corfu was evacuated by the Normans, the General maintained many other islands as his personal possessions. The islanders were tolerant of the Norman occupation that freed them of the heavy Byzantine hearth tax.

The stronghold on the island had been moved to the area of the Old Fort in the 10th century and the town was known as Korifo, which means "summit" after the twin peaks there. It is thought to be from this name that the present day "Corfu" derives.

Possession was to change hands many times and it had theoretically been awarded to Venice when the territories of the defeated Byzantine empire were divided up amongst the allies. However, the Despot Michael I Angelos maintained an occupation which was to last through the reign of four rulers until the island was awarded as a dowry in the marriage of the daughter of Michael

II Angelos to Manfred Hohenstaufer, ruler of Sicily, in 1257. Thus it became entangled in the Italian political struggle between the Pope and the Holy Roman Empire. Eventually the victorious Pontiff gave the island to a French prince in return for aid in his campaign.

The Venetian period

Life under the Despots had been comfortable for the Corfiots, with low taxation and complete religious freedom. The Angevin rule which placed 24 baronies on the island from 1267 to 1386 had the opposite effect and when in 1386, the Venetians took advantage of the Angevins' decline and, following a General Assembly, took over the island, they were treated as liberators although the people were to become serfs and the church did not regain complete freedom until the Russo-Turkish alliance took Corfu in 1798.

During this time there were two devastating attacks by the Turks: the first in 1537 saw the 4,000 strong garrison decimated by disease and starvation. When the Turks, who had suffered a similar fate, were finally repulsed, they burned the entire island before leaving and took with them some 20,000 slaves to be sold at Constantinople. Colonists of refugees from other cities overrun by the Turks quickly swelled the numbers and the New Fort was built between 1576 and 1588 to strengthen the defences. With the loss of Crete in 1669, Corfu gained in its importance to the Venetians.

The second assault was in 1716 when 30,000 infantry and 3,000 cavalry landed at Gouvia, and various parts of the city fell and were recaptured by the defence forces of 8,000 men, comprising Germans, Italians, Slavs and Greeks led by Count Von Der Schulenberg. After six weeks of fighting both sides were greatly weakened and it was feared that the Turks were about to launch a final assault on the now vulnerable defences. The next day saw a deserted enemy camp as the army had retreated, either because of their recall to aid in an attack on Venice or the miraculous intervention of St Spiridonas, whichever version takes your fancy.

Attacks by the Turks weren't the only troubles to beset the island and in 1629 and 1673 whole villages were wiped out by plague. Again the saint is said to have saved the island. Between 1463 and 1718, Venice was engaged in no fewer than seven wars with the Ottoman Empire and the drain on its resources was so great that in the latter years, despite having sold titles to the wealthy merchants who then had a place in the Assemblies and their names entered in the Golden Books, the Provveditore Generale Del Levant in charge of the island was so poor that he was reduced to hiring his furniture and cutlery from a local Jewish firm! During this time scholar priests Nikiforos Theotokis and Evyenios Voulgarios became the first to teach in Demotic Greek.

The French take over

Bonaparte saw the Ionian Islands as essential to his plans for the Mediterranean and Egyptian campaign and sent 2000 men who succeeded in capturing the islands within a few months. Having taken possession the French were at first popular as they chipped the wings of the symbolic Lions of St Mark and allowed the people to burn the hated Golden Books, planting victory trees throughout the island. This popularity was not to last, however, as the French mocked the priesthood and the soldiers were not paid but left to loot and pillage from the islanders. The last straw was when the much hated Jews were granted equal rights with the Orthodox citizens and the alliance with Ali Pasha of Ioannina angered the people.

In 1798, at the same time as the island came under siege from the Russo-Turkish alliance, the Corfiots started an uprising and the French were forced to bombard Mandouki where the rebels had congregated. Only Corfu of the Ionians had a sufficiently large garrison to hold off defeat until 1799, when the fellow Orthodox Russians restored the full rights of the church to the delighted people, who managed to overcome their distaste of the Turkish part of the matter. The troops had all left by 1801 and a Septinsular Republic under control of the Tsar had been formed. In his position as Secretary, the young Count John Kapodistrias urged his masters to allow the islands to aid the mainland that was under Turkish occupation.

All was not calm during this period, quite the contrary, and in 1802 two passing British frigates were called in to help put down riots and insurrection. The force was led by Count Mocenigo who remained behind as Russian Plenipotentiary until 1807. Various new constitutions were drawn up by Kapodistrias in an unsuccessful attempt to satisfy the people, who still maintained the divisions they had formed during the times of the Peloponnesian War.

In 1803 Britain and France were at war and once again Napoleon saw Corfu and its neighbours as the key to his success. The second occupation was less despised and General Donzelot's name is still found on a street in the town as he founded the Ionian Academy and brought printing presses to the island. By 1809 the British had retaken all the islands except Corfu and Paxos, the former of which had at least 40,000 men garrisoned there. A blockade was commenced but as soon the two British frigates were out of range, an armada of small boats from Albania rushed across the channel bringing supplies. Paxos fell in 1814 to the 2nd regiment of the Duke of York's Greek Light Infantry, among whose officers numbered Theodoros Kolokotronis who later became a leader in the war of Independence.

A British protectorate

The British protectorate from 1815 to 1864 brought good and bad to the island. The main bone of contention was the High Commissioners, the first of whom, Sir Thomas Maitland had complete control of the islands under the transparent cover of an Ionian Parliament, to which he appointed the members and which, as a last resort, he had power to dissolve.

Kapodistrias continued to press the British to allow the Ioanians to aid the mainland in their struggle to oust the Turks. The British continued to reopen the Ionian Academy, build roads, drainage systems, hospitals and palaces, but the islanders were not impressed. The constitution was liberalised in 1848 by Lord Seaton who at last freed the press. This prompted a renewed fervour and a convenient medium for the call for union with the mainland. William Gladstone, who had been appointed Lord High Commissioner Extraordinary, proposed further changes in 1858 in an attempt to appease the people. But they were having none of it and made a formal plea for union.

Union with Greece

When Greece in 1862 dethroned King Otto, the British found a face-saving way of handing over the islands and first insisted that a monarch acceptable to both countries be placed on the throne. Prince William of Denmark became King George I of the Hellenes in 1864 and a year later the British left with the proviso that Greece should remain militarily neutral, to which end the defences of the Old Fort and other strongholds were blown up.

The post-British era has seen further troubles for Corfu. The island was twice bombarded by Mussolini's forces. The first occasion was in 1923 in retaliation for the assassination on the Albanian border of an Italian delegate. The Italian occupation in 1941 was ended only when it was taken over by the Germans in 1943. The Jewish population that had grown to one in every nine citizens in 1889 was all but wiped out during this time, although a synagogue still remains in Kerkyra.

Under the Junta no controls were placed on the building of hotels and other constructions for the tourist industry. This began in about 1958 on Corfu, the island being a more likely choice for the development than its unfortunate neighbours which had experienced great destruction by the earthquake of 1953.

Mythology

Homer told of a people known as the Phaiakes or Phaeacians — a rich, happy and peaceful race that inhabited the island and largely occupied themselves singing and dancing.

A favourite of the gods, King Nausithoos had led his people to Scheria (Corfu) to escape from the harassment by the Cyclopes. Within his fine city the king married and had two sons: Rhexnor and Alkinoos, the latter of which married the daughter of the former and succeeded the throne. The palace of this enchanted land was comprised largely of precious metals and the gods held back most of the winds to protect the extensive vineyards and orchards there.

Jason and his Argonauts en route to return Medea to her father, the King of Colchis, visited the island. Dallying too long there, Jason married the maid and rendered the completion of the mission impossible. The couple and their crew were then forced to stay forever rather than face the anger of the bride's father.

The islanders were master ship builders and the vessels went one better than today's automatic steering gear as they needed neither captain nor crew to reach their destinations! In becoming known for aiding less fortunate sailors, they angered the sea god Poseidon, who threatened to surround the city with high mountains. One of those to benefit from this early version of RNLI was Odysseus who after two days in the sea was washed up on a shore that has kept many historians and archeologists busy in the attempt to identify it.

Where ever the location, Odysseus fell asleep exhausted and naked under some bushes. The goddess Athina in her customary role as protector of our hero, now enters the action. She rushed to the palace of Alkinoos and in the guise of a friend of the Princess Nausikaa, admonished her in a dream for not yet having washed the linen of her dowry for the approaching marriage.

After loading the laundry on a wagon, the Princess and her maids set off for the river. While waiting for the articles to dry on the stones, they took the opportunity for a swim. All the giggling hadn't yet awakened Odysseus so Athina caused one of the girls playing ball to misjudge her aim and in the attempts to retrieve the object, she disturbed him. Modestly holding a tree branch in front of him that must have done little to improve his bedraggled appearance, Odysseus approached the females who all scattered in panic except the Princess. Given courage by Athina, she stayed to hear the exceedingly polite explanation of his problems and decided that he must be a favourite of Zeus to have survived so much.

For some reason she declined to transport and introduce him to the palace herself and many allusions are made to a romance between them. Instead she left her servants to help him clean himself up a bit and suggested that he present himself on his knees to her mother Arete who, if sympathetic, would aid him. This he did and when questioned did not reveal his name but denied that he was a god.

It was arranged that a ship should be put at his disposal the next day to take him home and the evening was spent in a jolly good knees up, including the telling of epic stories from the Trojan war which had apparently reached the island faster than Odysseus himself, who was still trying to get home. In tears at the accounts, he told them who he was and took over the narrative.

The next morning the ship set sail and while he was once again asleep, he was gently lifted onto his home shore and the Phaeacians left him there on Ithaka. The furious Poseidon turned the returning ship to stone and it is said to be still there at Pondikonissi, or alternatively near Paleokastritsa.

TWENTY THREE

Paxos

Population: 2,500   *Highest point: 270m*
Area: 19 sq km   *Hotel beds: 164*

Among the smallest of the seven permanently inhabited Ionian islands, and no more than ten kilometres from one end to the other, Paxos has been endowed with far more than a fair share of natural beauty. Perhaps of more significance it remains unspoilt by human over-exploitation and may well stay that way, owing to a chronic shortage of fresh water and a long but casual acquaintance with tourism from the many visitors that have made the excursion on a day trip from Corfu, whence they can glimpse its character without depleting its resources.

Here, unbelievably turquoise seas, lace edged with white beaches that have been likened to those of the Caribbean, still adjoin olive groves rather than hotel complexes. The arriving visitors descend from the ferry to the sound of the tired engines and the screams of the gulls, not cries of "Rooms, you want rooms?"

From a distance Paxos appears every bit as green as Corfu and it is easy from this angle to doubt what you may have heard of the need for supplies of fresh water to be brought from the mainland until a few years ago. The truth is only apparent when you walk among the olive trees and notice the comparative absence of vegetation at the base of the trunks where on Corfu would be found a tangle of weeds and wild flowers. The coming of modern technology in the form of the black plastic netting now used to collect the biannual olive harvest has led to the many miles of low stone walls, which previously limited both the rolling of the fruit and the erosion of the earth, being allowed to fall into disrepair and the winter rains to wash away the precious soil.

At the port, where the yellow dinosaurs have gouged into the hillside to prepare for a wider access road, the geology of the island can be seen in the thin veins of rich, nearly black earth amongst the

PAXOS

Scale 1:84 000

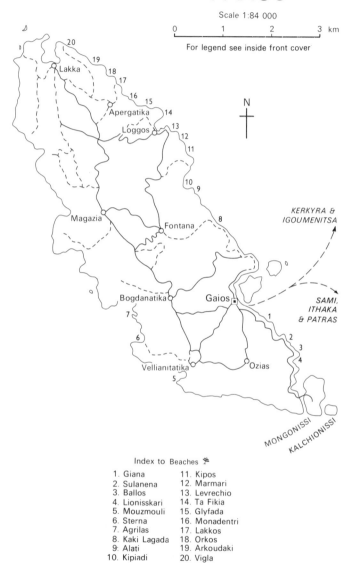

For legend see inside front cover

N

KERKYRA &
IGOUMENITSA

SAMI,
ITHAKA
& PATRAS

Lakka
Apergatika
Loggos
Magazia
Fontana
Bogdanatika
Gaios
Vellianitatika
Ozias

MONGONISSI
KALCHIONISSI

Index to Beaches

1. Giana
2. Sulanena
3. Ballos
4. Lionisskari
5. Mouzmouli
6. Sterna
7. Agrilas
8. Kaki Lagada
9. Alati
10. Kipiadi
11. Kipos
12. Marmari
13. Levrechio
14. Ta Fikia
15. Glyfada
16. Monadentri
17. Lakkos
18. Orkos
19. Arkoudaki
20. Vigla

thick layers of impermeable rock. The same strata rise to form the cliffs of the west coast, magnificent in their sheerness. More exposed here to the elements, the rock has been eroded to form sea caves and towering obelisks now isolated from the mainland.

It is dificult to imagine where all the inhabitants of Paxos live as, although the maps show many villages, on exploration they prove to be at most half a dozen houses by the side of the road with perhaps one tiny shop. On the outskirts will be found ruined olive presses and the shells of dwellings that bear witness to a different lifestyle in days gone by. There is, however, no atmosphere of decay or air of gloom about these semi-derelict villages: they have a feel of simply waiting for their eventual renovation rather than for oblivion.

Another mistake it is easy to make regarding the landscape of Paxos, seen from a distance, is that the land is raised and flat. The olive groves camouflage a series of hills and valleys that ensure you always seem to be going either up or down hill!

The fishing fleet has been reduced in size over recent years but the daily catch is still sold in the early morning hours in the market place in Gaios, the island's capital, while the rest of the population are largely dependent on the olives and, to a much lesser extent, tourism for their livelihood.

Perhaps being in such close proximity to Corfu (seven nautical miles from tip to tip and thirty-two from port to port) has enabled the people of Paxos to witness the drawbacks of mass tourism and a concerted effort has so far been made both to conserve the character of the island and to encourage an "up-market" visitor. Even land prices are four times those of Corfu and so retiring to one of those tumbledown houses isn't as cheap as you might expect or hope it to be.

"Paxos" is an anglicised form of what should be "Paxi". When Paxi, Antipaxi and the islets are being referred to, the plural "Ta Paxus" (which rhymes with goose) will be used by the locals.

Arrival by sea

During the months of the high season, Gaios port is a stop for the Italy to Greece ferries of the Seven Islands Line's vessel *Cephalonian Sky* and therefore connects directly with Patras (9hrs), Kefallonia (8hrs) and Ithaka (5hrs). Outside of these months it is necessary to change ferries at Igoumenitsa (mainland) or Kerkyra

As the sign says, you can go and see the 'Blue Grot' in this little caique that the express boat owners scorn, saying it takes all day to make the return trip. In the background is the old residency of the High Commissioner, a three-storey building now taken over by a holiday company.

(Corfu) to link up with the Greece to Italy/Yugoslavia routes. Tickets must be purchased in advance from the company's agent in the main street in Gaios or from any of the travel offices in Lakka or Loggos.

A smaller car ferry *c/f Kerkyra,* of the type used on most of the domestic routes, crosses from Kerkyra via Igoumenitsa (4hrs) on Mondays, Wednesdays and Fridays, increasing to daily in the high season. Hot and cold drinks are available plus a limited selection of snacks. Indoor seating capacity and the two toilets can soon become inadequate for the high demand placed on them in the summer and during the "rush hours". Tickets from any travel office.

At the end of the tiny concrete ramp opposite the Agricultural Bank of Greece on the quayside in Gaios, the *Kamelia* and the *f/b Kerkyra* (just to confuse the issue!) load and dock overnight. The *Kamelia* departs at 07.30 to the following timetable:

Monday	Loggos—Lakka—Kerkyra
Tuesday	Mourtos (Sivota on the mainland)—Kerkyra
Wednesday	Lakka—Kerkyra
Thursday	Mourtos—Kerkyra
Friday	Lakka—Kerkyra

This little ship can hold six cars at a pinch. The variety of different types of chairs in the lounge makes it look rather quaint inside but I am sure a different perspective is seen by those who travel in bad weather as the seats aren't fastened to the floor!

The *f/b Kerkyra,* a passenger only vessel, also departs from here to the following timetable:

Monday	17.00	Lakka—Loggos—Gaios
Tuesday	13.00	Mourtos—Gaios
Wednesday	13.00	Lakka—Gaios
Thursday	13.00	Mourtos—Gaios
Friday	14.00	Mourtos—Gaios
Saturday	13.00	Lakka—Gaios

Timetables for the departure of both of the above ships are posted in all three of the island's ports, outside cafés, on notice boards and on the quayside and it would be wise to check the above details in advance of your departure. Bear in mind that the smaller vessels are more prone to cancellation due to bad weather. Tickets are purchased on board.

Out of season the fast passenger boats *Paxos Dolphin* and *Pegasus* make the crossing between Kerkyra and Paxos on alternate days to the larger car ferry and rising to twice daily in the summer. The journey time is cut to an hour and the fares are double. These boats leave from the quayside in Gaios and occasionally call at one of the other two ports. Check locally for up-to-the-minute details.

Paxos is connected with Parga on the mainland and Kavos on Corfu by excursion vessels but the round-about route taken and the fact that it is expensive make it an unlikely choice for getting to Paxos.

Antipaxos

Twenty-seater speed boats leave hourly for Antipaxos during the times of year when there are enough people wanting to be transported to and from its beaches. Exact departure times are chalked on a board next to the boats opposite the square in Gaios.

Athens—Paxos bus

There are two weekly departures from Athens via Mourtos and connecting with the *f/b Kamelia.* Fare 3,450drs plus 800drs for the boat ticket. The travel office is at 2 Kavala on the corner of Leoforos Athinas. Tel. (Athens) 01 522 6031 or (Paxos) 0662 31245/31561.

Centres of population

Gaios

Gaios (pronounced like the christian name "Guy" + oss and with the stress on the first syllable) is the island's capital and principal port.

When the ferry has departed and seemingly left you at a building site in the middle of nowhere, you need to round the last bend of the road as it curves along a parallel course to the edge of Aghios Nikolaos island opposite. Then you'll catch your first glimpse of the incredibly picturesque waterfront, an experience never to be forgotten.

The narrow channel between the two islands is a deep green reflection of the trees on the far bank. Together with the architecture of the pastel painted ornate three storey houses, the effect is possibly Venetian but certainly more of a riverside

The old British residency of the High Commissioner has been redecorated as far as the ground floor, which is used by a holiday company. To my mind the top two storeys look much more attractive.

settlement than a coastal port. Never was there such a setting for the gaily decorated caiques as moored in front of the square, where the little white painted church is half concealed behind delicate oleanders. The elegance of the yachts pales in comparison.

The size of the village isn't at first apparent until you eventually realise that what seems to be a large selection of shops is really the same arcade that you have passed at least twice before from different directions. The side streets, large and small, all join up in front of one of the few olive presses still in operation and where the musty smell of the piles of brown waste mark the edge of the village and the beginning of the countryside beyond.

Mongonissi, just over two kilometres south of Gaios, can no longer claim to be an island as the once shallow stretch of sea between it and Paxos has been filled in and now a road wide enough to take cars crosses from the main island. This unsurfaced road makes unfulfilled promises as it leads uphill, past the turn off to the taverna and some dog kennels, before coming to an abrupt halt in the middle of nowhere. There are neither houses nor beaches on this islet but it is a popular evening destination.

To the south east of Mongonissi, still unannexed and likely to remain that way, is what the map prints as Kalchionissi but the way the Paxiots pronounce it it sounds more like "Kaltsonissi", which means "Sock-island"!

Loggos
Small even by Paxos standards, this lovely little port half way between Gaios and Lakka is comprised of a handful of houses, two travel agents, three tavernas and two bars in a natural harbour. A small stretch of sandy beach is backed by the incongruous ruins of a factory that has produced at various times cognac, oil and soap, and whose chimney and exterior walls look as if they have been transported straight out of Dickensian industrial Britain. Not for much longer however as the same building is destined to be face lifted in its transformation into an apartment complex. With a less optimistic future are the two disused windmills along the coast to the north.

Lakka
The outskirts (if the word isn't too pretentious for such a small settlement) of Lakka have considerable construction work in progress and of course this does little to enhance the appearance of the area. Apart from one or two appealing scenes of picturesque balconies, and places where the crumbling paintwork of pastel walls

The harbour at Lakka where except for the brief visits by the excursion boats from Corfu, the port has a sleepy feel about it.

resembles scenes found on the postcards on sale at all the souvenir shops, the village is nothing to write home about, especially when you have already been spoilt by the charms of Gaios and Loggos. On the water's edge the quality takes an about turn: when the whole area is seen from the heights beyond the preposterously blue sea in the bay that is its setting, it is one of the most inspiringly beautiful sights in Greece.

Thankfully there is still enough space along the beaches that line the bay to accommodate those that will arrive to fill the rooms now being built, and so far the facilities in the village are in keeeping with the character of the area. Of the three ports this is probably the one most likely to become over commercialised and so we can only hope that the water shortage will check the amount of development allowed — a thought to make us more tolerant of those salty showers!

Magazia

Magazia means "shops", and it isn't hard to see how this village got its name. It must have been a convenient location for the islanders from the three equidistant ports to take produce to sell and to buy supplies and services from others gathered for the same purpose when, in days gone by, transport was a donkey or meant an early start for the walk.

You may be lucky enough to see an ancient trade pursued in its traditional form at the old forge, or perhaps the owner will take that old car that looks as if it came straight out of a Garbo movie for a spin. Anyway the café is a pleasant place to sit and wait for the world to go by.

The missing villages

Despite a further twenty seven villages marked impressively on the map, there isn't anything there to cause you to think other than that Anemogianatika, Kondogianatika, Arvanitakeika and other such tongue twisters are the names of houses rather than of settlements. I am convinced that Vlachopoulatika is the name of the donkey that I came across in the appropriate area shown on the map!

Road system

The standard of the road surface varies greatly from newly laid tarmac to murderous dirt tracks of large loose stones. From the port and along the quayside into Gaios, the concrete has, to start with, just a few small potholes in its surface but these develop towards the main square into a veritable lunar landscape.

The roads connecting Gaios, Loggos and Lakka are all asphalted, with the exception of a two kilometre stretch just outside Lakka on the more westerly of the two routes to Gaios.

Secondary roads are often concrete with shallow grooves drawn across them to aid drainage and provide additional road holding. These tracks are found on some of the steepest gradients and in places it is almost impossible to get a motorbike around the bend without "jack-knifing"!

The worst stretch of all is obviously destined to become tarmac and leads down from Fontana to the port, providing a quicker route than that from Bogdanatika.

Buses

Timetables are displayed prominently in all the villages but the time of the last bus should be checked with the driver unless your schedule is flexible.

07.30	Lakka—Loggos—Gaios
10.15	Gaios—Loggos—Lakka
11.00	Lakka—Loggos—Gaios
13.30	Gaios—Loggos—Lakka
14.15	Lakka—Gaios
17.30	Gaios—Loggos—Lakka
18.30	Lakka—Loggos—Gaios.

There is no service on Sundays and holidays. The vehicle is blue and entry is by the front door where you pay the driver.

Taxis

The island has five taxis each equipped with C.B. radio. Telephone 31280 should you not find one outside the Agricultural Bank in Gaios or the aquarium in Lakka. (You could hardly fail to see a taxi in Loggos if there is one there at the time!) Approximate fares: Gaios-Loggos 700drachmas; Loggos-Lakka 400drachmas; Gaios-Lakka 700drachmas; Gaios-port 250drachmas; Gaios-Moggonissi 400drachmas. An additional charge is made for items of luggage and during unsocial hours.

A pleasant alternative are the sea taxis: small speed boats that make the trip in about the same time as the cars. Prices are according to how many people want to go, enquire before embarking. You will see the "Taxi" signposts looking incongruous on the harbour edge, or pinned to the trunk of a tree on a lonely beach!

Petrol

As is the case on most small islands, Paxos has short periods when there is no petrol available. Recent strikes have worsened the problem as, if they occur on the day when the fuel boat is due to make its visit then the island must wait until the next scheduled trip. The rent-a-bike businesses seem to have adequate supplies for their vehicles but they can get into serious trouble for selling fuel. The only petrol station is 200m along the road to Vellianitatika from Gaios. Open from 07.30 to 13.00 and on Tuesday, Thursday and Friday evenings from 17.00 to 20.00hrs. Closed all day Sunday.

Maps
Visitors are not exactly spoilt for choice here but Toubi's map is easy to use and largely accurate. Paxos, Antipaxos and the relative position to the mainland are detailed, plus a short legend.

Vehicle rental
All three ports have rent-a-bike agencies with a good selection of large and small motorbikes, mopeds and even bicycles for the more energetic.

Car rental is arranged through the travel offices who liaise with Corfu or the mainland for the appropriate vehicle to be dispatched. This entails an additional expense on what is already a pricey business. If you wish to hire in the peak months, as much notice as possible should be given to enable space to be reserved on the car ferries. These can become booked up for many days at a time, as can the cars themselves during the August holidays.

Accommodation

While my initial reaction was pleasant suprise at not being fought over by various room owners all vying for my custom, it would have been useful to have been approached by someone with a knowledge of where accommodation could most easily be found, especially as it was hot and my luggage heavy: but this was not to be.

In the full season it is not uncommon for all accommodation to become full and it would be much wiser to have made arrangements before leaving the UK unless you are prepared to be flexible and go elsewhere if necessary. See Chapter 3 for details of how to book from home. The first thing to do outside of the silly-season is to decide in which of the three ports you want to stay.

Gaios
Walk or take a taxi the 600m to the village where one of the first buildings you come to will be the "E" class **Hotel San Georgio** where, at the top of a very long flight of steps are clean rooms with shared bathroom facilities. Further on you come to a few villas and the first of the travel offices, all of which have details of the more up-market accommodation in pensions and villas. They will also call on your behalf the **Hotel Paxos Beach,** whose fifty bungalow type rooms are located 1,500m from the village centre. This method means that you don't have to deal directly with the ignorant desk

clerk there in order to ascertain the availability of a room in this strictly half-board hotel.

Rooms in private houses are numerous but are largely along one of the side streets that doesn't immediately attract your attention. Proceed along the sea front until you come to the post office then head up the little side street and turn right where the flag pole marks the doorway of the police station. A list should be available here of all the rooms to let, but should is the operative word as on 10 June they still hadn't received the current year's details from NTOG. From last year's list they were very willing to telephone on my behalf but once the owners understand where the call is coming from, you are instantly persona non grata and all replies are non commital! Continuing left and up hill, all of the houses in this street have "to let" signs in English and German. On the sea front road, the second red house from the square has accommodation for rent.

Loggos

It may be more difficult to find a room or apartment here as the limited number are soon snapped up by the holiday companies. Enquire at the Loggos Tours travel office where one of the partners is an Englishman who has been running the business there since 1982.

The port of Loggos. The houses in the background have rooms for rent.

Plans have been approved for the conversion of the old soap factory to apartment units with a courtyard and museum within the complex.

Lakka

The construction work on the outskirts of the village is obviously going to provide more accommodation of one type or another. At the moment the only hotels are the "E" class **Ilios,** a rather unattractively decorated three-storey building in the centre of the village, and the **Lefkothea** adjacent to it.

Houses displaying "room to let" signs are found along the road that leads northwards within the village towards the lighthouse, but the best bet is to enquire at the office of Routsi's Holidays Ltd on the northern edge of the quayside.

Camping

There are no camping facilities on either Paxos or Antipaxos and neither is it tolerated.

Water

The water used for showers in most of the accommodation is so salty that it would be easy to believe it had come directly from the sea. This has a disastrous effect on all but the most resilient hair types and a large supply of conditioner should be taken with you or purchased on arrival.

Where to eat

Only in Gaios would it be possible during a week long holiday to be unable to try all the restaurants and tavernas there.

One of the few that had a selection of hot ready cooked dishes *(figh ée tis casa róh lez)* rather than the usual steak and *souvlaki* etc is **Spiros** opposite the cigarette wholesalers/Commercial Bank of Greece to the right of the square with your back to the sea.

Should you tire of Greek recipes, a very good chicken curry is served at the Gaios restaurant **Alexandros,** between the bike rental office and the Agricultural Bank of Greece. Those undeterred by the advertisements depicting congenial looking lobsters marching with placards that read "Vive lobster" will no doubt delight at choosing which of those in the tanks at **Mongonissi Taverna** should be put into the boiling water!

The **Gaios Grill,** just before the olive press, has an assortment of tender meats spit roasted over charcoal. Don't be deterred by the appearance of the *kondoh sóo vlee* which bears a remarkable resemblence to the charcoal beneath but is in fact well cooked pork and thoroughly delicious.

Disappointing desserts

In the interests of thorough research (of course) I sampled the "doughnuts with icecream" seen advertised at all three of the restaurant/cafés in the square in Gaios. This dish is traditional in Greece and often eaten for breakfast! The doughnuts *(loo koo már dez)* are small balls of crispy batter over which honey is generously poured and either icecream or cream make an excellent topping.

Imagine my disappointment when presented with a plateful of potential cannonballs with a crowning obscenity of green icecream and red vegetable dye poured over the resulting mess! It seems, however, that they did have some reason for adulterating the original as I heard coos of envy from a neighbouring table.

Nightlife

I was suprised to learn that there were only three discotheques on the island and flabbergasted to find only one open; hence the interior decor and quality of entertainment at the Aloni, 500m out of Lakka on the west road, and the Galazia, 300m out of Gaios on the road to Vellianitatika, must remain a mystery.

Phoenix Disco, a new and well designed building on the hillside above the port road 800m from the centre of Gaios, is located far enough from the habitations to avoid causing a nuisance and hence the volume of the music is extremely loud. The wood panelled ceiling, generous number of artificial plants and a large attractive balcony area provide a very romantic setting, especially when, as was the case when I visited, they have laid on a full moon to enhance the view over the bay to the glittering sea below. Reasonably priced for the facilities offered. See if you can spot the waiter who served you your evening meal, they are all there! Open from 23.00hrs on Saturdays (possibly plus Fridays in the busier months).

At **Mongonissi Taverna,** the waiters (and sometimes the lobsters) perform Greek dancing which you are encouraged to join in. **The Piano Bar** boasts piano music at a pleasant quayside setting in Loggos.

At Loggos, a lovely setting for a relaxing drink in the shade.

What to see and do

Walks

Along the edge of the coast and the roads, major and minor, those who enjoy strolls or hikes will find plenty to please the eye in the landscape of what is a small enough island to thoroughly explore in a short holiday. There are reputedly three books of detailed walks on Paxos and Antipaxos but I only came across one on the island and another in Corfu: *Rambles Around Paxos* by and from Loggos Tours Ltd, and *Landscapes of Paxos* by Noel Rochford, published by Sunflower Books, London.

Gaios Aquarium

From the size of the building, I expected a ridiculously small exhibition but I emerged over an hour later impressed by the enterprise and thoroughly enjoyed my visit. The tanks, into which run a continual flow of sea water and air, hold not only a variety of species of fish but also of sea anemones that I haven't seen in any of the international standard aquaria. Perhaps this is because at the end of each season the exhibits are returned to the sea and there is an abundant supply of replacements should anything begin to look "poorly". An evil looking conger eel, disconcertingly labelled as living in depths of under two metres, allows the owner, Michalis Dalietos, to stroke it! Rather him than me! A colossal spider crab clacks around the tank and the expression of the octopus makes you very sorry that you managed to acquire the taste with your evening ouzo. Titbits of food dropped into the tank remain unseen by the short-sighted, sharklike dogfish but once the scent of the meat permeates, there is a flurry of activity until it is gulped down. Possessing much better eyesight and with a disturbing but endearingly human expression is the Kaponi or Gurnard fish which follows the course of a finger moved near the tank to point at one of his fellow exhibits. When someone took a photograph, I will swear that he posed and I began to feel uncertain of who should be which side of the glass! Admission 250drs, free for small children. Open from 11.00 to 17.00hrs seven days a week all season.

Aquarium Lakka
Similar enthusiasm has been expressed over the exhibits here and photographs displayed outside would seem to indicate that they are identical but the opening hours are limited to 11.00-12.30 and 17.00-18.30 Monday to Saturday.

Excursions
Around-the-island trips are made independently from all the ports daily at 10-10.30hrs, except on days when even a moderate breeze in the east can mean that there is a swell in the west which makes conditions unsuitable for the speed boats. Speed is the operative word and it is sometimes difficult to work your camera while trying not to get either bounced overboard or your precious equipment soaked in spray. High speed films are a must if you want to get shots of the coastline. Disappointingly, the fantastic blues of the water in the coves aren't visible from the sea.

The sea caves leave you commenting on the seamanship of the captain rather than anything remarkable within, except a smell of sulphur, and unless someone is resourceful enough to have brought along a torch, there isn't really a lot to see as the much heard about seals are rather unreliable. Even the inspiring tale of Papanikolaos cave being named after a Greek submarine that hid there, thereby foiling enemy attempts to find it after gallant raids on their fleets, is scorned by others as pure fantasy. Well if it isn't true, it should be!

Best seen from this angle are the cliffs of Ermitis, the Tripitos

Ortholithos seen from inside Petriti cave on the western coast of the island.

arch and Ortholithos, the proud finger of rock left in isolation by the erosion the elements have caused.

The whole tour takes a little over two hours including a fifteen minute stop at Lakka. There is the option of disembarking at either of the beaches of Antipaxos and returning later by means of certain of the express boats, the times of which will be explained to you. Fare 1,500 drs.

Kavos on Corfu is the destination twice a week of the little *Anna Maria* but why anyone would wish to make the trip this way round is beyond my imagination.

A trip to Antipaxos hardly qualifies as an excursion as the journey only takes ten minutes. Stops are made at Vrika and Voutoumi beaches and those who are slightly unsteady on their feet should note that the jetty at Voutoumi floats and therefore rocks quite alarmingly while the rocks at Vrika are very uneven on the last few feet before the water's edge. 500 drs return. Boats leave hourly from Gaios and the last return from Antipaxos is at 17.00hrs.

If you wish to make a sailing trip to **Lefkes, Parga** or **Mourtos,** mini cruises of both one and two day duration are made from Lakka on the thirty-foot Hamara. Routsi's Holidays in Lakka will supply details.

Tennis
There is one floodlit hardcourt 200m from Lakka on the west road to Gaios. Enquiries at Planos Holidays office in Lakka, tel.31744.

Watersports
Water skiing, windsurfing and paragliding are available at Loggos and Lakka. For those interested in specialist watersports holidays, see Chapter 3

Diving
For those with licenses of whatever standard, tuition, equipment and transportation to diving sites are provided by Paxos Diving, whose centre is easily spotted by the rack of wet suits outside and near to the rent-a-bike shop in the east end of the port at Lakka.

Boat hire
Speed boats can be hired on a daily and weekly basis from all three ports. Costs are around 4,000drs per day plus petrol.

Museums

Before long there will be a small museum of artifacts from the factory in Loggos once its conversion to an apartment complex is completed. A similar project is under way for a museum to house local folkloric items opposite the aquarium in Lakka.

Beaches

The expression "pebbly beach", to my mind conjures up unattractive images of coastal stretches, like Lowestoft for example, and while I am really quite fond of that part of the country, I wouldn't travel across Europe to seek a similar landscape! The smooth white stones and pebbles that form the border between an irresistible sea and someone's allotment on Paxos, are much more inviting to stretch out on and soak up some of that glorious sunshine!

If you really must have sand then head for Antipaxos where the two beaches that the boats call at both have plenty of sand between the water and the stones on the inner edge.

Part of the fun of a Paxos holiday is finding your own beach, whether on foot or from a hired speed boat, but I will provide some suggestions here.

In Gaios itself is a tiny stretch that gets full up with Greek families with small children. Between here and Mongonissi are the coves of **Giana, Sulanena, Ballos** and **Lionisskari,** all of which can be reached without too much imagination and are visible from the road, with the exception of Sulanena which must be reached via the grounds of the Paxos Beach Hotel who have a small bar down there and permit your entry from 09.00-24.00hrs.

The south coast is composed of low rocks that can hold no appeal except to snorkellers who may have to wait a long time for weather mild enough to make it possible to swim there. It is forbidden for rented boats to go further than Mongonissi, which precludes their use to reach those two tempting beaches at **Mouzmouli** and **Sterna** that provide yet another reason for wishing you had your own yacht. Never mind, there is **Agrilas** beach that can be reached on foot from the turn off on a bend just before Vellianitatika (alias the little café!). On the rare occasions when the wind is from the east, this beach should provide shelter.

What the west coast lacks, the east coast makes up for. North of Gaios is **Kaki Lagada** close to the coastal road out of the port, just before it turns inland and becomes nearly impassable. Between here

Mouzmouli Bay, one of two such lovely beaches that can be reached only by sea in an area that requires permission from the port police to visit as the seas are hazardous.

and Loggos are the coves of **Alati** (salt), **Kipiadi, Kipos** (garden), **Marmari** (marble) and **Levrechio.** In Loggos port sea weed grows in the shallows and the effect is rather uninviting. North from the port are **Ta Fikia** ("sea weed", but there isn't any!) **Glyfada, Monadentri** (only tree) and on to **Lakkos** and **Orkos** beaches with some water sport and refreshment facilities. Continuing north, **Arkoudaki** and **Vigla** can be reached with determination and care or by boat.

Turning into the natural harbour of Lakka by boat you can't appreciate the intensely beautiful colours of the sea within until you approach the shore or climb the rocks above. What is it: ultramarine, aquamarine, turquoise? There must be a word somewhere to convey how wonderfully BLUE it is! As if that isn't enough, nearly the whole area of the bay is skirted by beach. Should you be able to tear yourself away from the aforementioned, there are two small lonely coves a short way to the west.

Useful information

Banks
All three bank branches are in Gaios but the only one conspicuously sited is the Agricultural Bank of Greece which doesn't perform exchange operations for visitors. To the right (back to the sea) of the square and along the right hand side of the street there are a cigarette wholesalers and a decorators' supplies shop. This isn't as irrelevant as it might appear as within are respectively the Commercial and National Banks of Greece agencies. Shop hours are kept and the National Bank is unable to supply its customers with deposit and withdrawal facilities for those whose accounts are at branches other than Paxos or Kerkyra.

Post office
The only post office on the island is on the quayside in Gaios past the square. Open from 08.00 to 14.00 Monday to Friday. Shops selling postcards sell stamps at up to 10 per cent permitted surcharge.

Police
The police station in Gaios can be reached by going past the post office and down any of the side streets. Should the squad car not happen to be outside the door, the flags and brass plaque give its location away. I found the officers there very helpful and polite. Tel 31222.

Port police
Easily spotted on the quayside, the office is up the spiral staircase and on the first floor. Downstairs and just inside the door is an up-to-date chart of the regular weekly departures from all the ports. Tel 31259.

Customs
As Paxos is an official point of entry into Greece, there is a small customs office in one of the houses among the first buildings you reach coming from the new port.Tel 31676.

Doctors
There are two surgeries in Gaios and both are signposted in English. The large house with the verandah garden on the main street, tel: 31777, and the house on the corner of the square with the large "Surgery" sign, tel: 31466. Anyone with a serious problem is transported to the mainland or Corfu by helicopter.

Telephone office
The OTE is on the main street and next door to the Seven Islands Lines office. Open from 07.30-15.10 Monday to Saturday. See below.

Information
Travel offices are plentiful and exchange currency travellers and Eurocheques for a small fee plus offering a metered phone service.

Reading matter
New paperbacks, newspapers and magazines are easily found in all the ports. A fantastic selection including some classics and latest best sellers awaits anyone with a book to swop in the Loggos Tours office in Loggos. Most of the travel offices have at least a few books and surprisingly don't charge for the exchange service.

Laundry

Owing to the water shortages, there is neither a laundry nor dry cleaners on the island. If you wish to have someone wash your clothes for you, enquire at one of the hotels or travel offices for current details.

Historical background

As is to be expected of islands in such close proximity, the histories of Corfu and Paxos are almost identical including their being subject to frequent attacks by both Turkish and pirate raiders. The Venetians granted permission to the island's former owner, Baron Adam San Ipolitos, to build a castle on the islet of Aghios Nicholaos. Consequently, with Corfu, Paxos was one of the few areas never to have been subject to Turkish rule, although raids in 1537 and 1571 decimated the population. It is all the more suprising then that when impossibly high taxes were levied by Ioannis Avramis, to whose family the island had been given in 1513, Turkey was one of the destinations for the many islanders who emigrated to escape this economic persecution, which was to continue until a successful appeal was made to the General Provost of Corfu in 1675.

In 1807, when the French resumed their occupation which had been interrupted by the Russo-Turkish fleet's "liberation" and construction of an independent federal republic, their disrespect towards the church and favours bestowed on the Jewish population caused them to be resented by the islanders. The British embargo gave rise to a famine which in 1810, under the leadership of an infamous pirate, Captain Kefalos, inspired the Paxiots to rebel against the French. Once the governor had been killed and rioting had broken out, Kefalos arrived to take charge of the island but he was to do a quick about turn a few days later when the French fleet landed. Taking most of his followers and a considerable amount of booty with him, he fled to a happier fate than those of his supporters left behind, who were executed by the French, which did little to improve their popularity.

The British forces that captured the island in 1814 were largely commanded by Greek officers and no resistance was met.

Mythology firmly lays the credit for the creation of Paxos at Poseidon's feet but how it came about is the subject of two conflicting accounts. On a journey between Corfu and Levkas, the god became tired and wished to rest, which he was able to do after hitting the waves with his trident and causing the green and pleasant island to appear. Alternatively, in an early act of vandalism, he hit the southern tip of Corfu and the pieces that broke away were Paxos and Antipaxos, which he then used as a weekend retreat from those other tedious gods and as a love nest to which to take Amphitriti.

TWENTY FOUR

Antipaxos

With an area of just three square kilometres and a population of little over a hundred, Antipaxos really is a get-away-from-it-all location. Without even a small shop from which to purchase supplies and bearing in mind that the last boat full of day trippers from Paxos and Corfu leaves at five o'clock sharp, evening solitude is guaranteed. Within the walls of the individual plots, vines prosper and it is from these that the noted white and rosé wines are produced.

The houses are mostly of modern design and little appeal and the only surfaced road is from Aghios Emilianos to Agrapidia, but there are many stretches where it reverts to a dirt road again. The island's attraction lies in the two beaches of Vrika and Voutoumi, whose clear waters of irresistible hues have been listed amongst the world's most attractive. At Vrika the rocks that the boats dock next to are rather difficult to get your footing on but, unlike Paxos, there really is sand here and tavernas at both ends of the beach provide refreshments.

Further south and past the small cove of Mesovrika is the second and last beach whose taverna is at the top of a very, very long flight of steps and where the moussaka was awful. Here the pontoon that connects with the land rocks alarmingly and it is necessary to get a controlled rhythm going in order to cross it at any speed.

Exploring the island

I walked all the island routes and, discounting the taverna owners, sighted only four locals, all of whom were very friendly and supplied me with directions that managed to get me totally lost! The three maps I had with me did nothing to help either, as what looks like a road in print is in reality a two foot wide pass between two stone walls that are high enough to make it impossible for you to

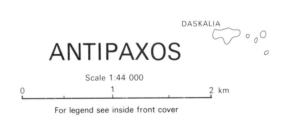

ANTIPAXOS

Scale 1:44 000

For legend see inside front cover

A little seen aspect of Antipaxos: the port at Agrapidia built in the sixties.

see if they are going to turn out to be dead ends (which they invariably did) or even in which direction they lead.

One of the islander's and a certain book of walks assured me that the lighthouse on the southern tip was only an hour away from Agrapidia, the island's manmade harbour where a pretty little beach is enhanced by the few boats and caiques moored there. After walking for ninety minutes, I crested a little hill and found that the lighthouse was at last in sight, another full hour's walk further on! My main concern was that I was now going to have a lot less time to explore than I had anticipated — until I realised that the road I was committed to taking had another kilometre at least of steep downhill over horribly sharp, loose stones that would have caused any self respecting mountain goat to watch its step. It was too late to turn back and I consider myself lucky to have got away with no more than hopelessly damaged knee tendons by the time I reached the bottom.

The island wasn't through with me yet and did nothing to reward my determination to press on to Vrika and not to take the tempting option of catching the last boat from Voutoumi after a long cool drink at the taverna there. Reluctantly I set off for Vrika (which means "I found" and must have been coined by someone after a similar experience to my own!).

Both on the open stretches, where black earth looking suspiciously like olive press waste crunches underfoot, and in the labyrinths of the walled alleyways where, infuriating as they are, you can't help but marvel at the patience and craftsmanship that has made a stable structure of so many small stones, the sun beats down unmercifully even in spring.

Every 100 metres a fork in the road appeared where the map said there shouldn't be one and I tried to mark these but I became less and less sure that I was in fact heading for the right place, as each time I had to make a choice of routes to take, there wasn't the help of Robert Frost's "road less travelled by" to influence my decision, just his "the passing there had worn them really about the same". By now I had the early signs of heat stroke and it must have been a pathetic looking piece of humankind that staggered eventually across Vrika beach and up to a waiter at the taverna to ask for a glass of water with a rather wild eyed expression and a hint of desperation in its voice!

As there was a whole fifteen minutes to spare before the last boat was due to leave and I had now finished my research for this volume, I decided to treat myself to a dip as enjoyed by other mortals but not, up to then, by me. With gay abandon I threw myself in and was heard to utter (hopefully not by small children) a similar exclamation to the one I used the first time I had my legs waxed! It was so cold! Lowestoft, all is forgiven!

Accommodation

It is possible to stay on Antipaxos but the arrangements are for houses and villas, not for rooms. Loggos Tours Ltd and Routsi's Holidays have secured accommodation there (see Chapter 3) but independant enquiries should be made at the tavernas or by using the one telephone line that then diversifies into twenty odd extension numbers: 31284.

Dionissos Vlahopoulos at the Voutoumi beach taverna has a house to rent and will be pleased to help those wanting to find accommodation if possible; but it should be remembered that most of the houses here are used as holiday if not weekend homes, and therefore are likely to be required by their owners in the high season, and that it will be difficult to track down the owners at other times.

Appendix A

The Greek Language

The main reason for including this chapter is that the effort of learning a few words of the language will be repaid many times by the reception you will get from the Greek people. Just to wish an islander "good morning" in his language is like paying him a compliment and although he may then assume that you speak fluent Greek and proceed to rattle on at top speed, you will be instantly accepted and liable to some of the very generous Greek hospitality.

Some of the smaller islands have very few English-speaking inhabitants and so a few of the most commonly used expressions may be helpful but a phrase book is a worthwhile investment and this chapter does not aim to replace them.

All Greek words in this book are spelt phonetically and not in the accepted English equivalent spelling. The syllable stress is very important in Greek and to put it in the wrong place can change the meaning completely. The accent denotes the syllable to be stressed.

The alphabet

The Greek alphabet is confusing because some of the letters that look like ours have a totally different sound:

A α alpha	apple		Ξ ξ ksee	ro<u>cks</u>
B β veta	ne<u>v</u>er		O o omikron	<u>o</u>n
Γ γ gamma	<u>y</u>ellow or <u>g</u>ap		Π π pee	<u>p</u>aper
Δ δ thelta	<u>th</u>en		P ρ roe	<u>r</u>oe
E ε epsillon	<u>e</u>nter		Σ σ sigma	<u>s</u>and
Z ζ zita	<u>z</u>ip		T τ taff	<u>t</u>iff

H η ita	ch**ee**se	Υ υ ipsilon	pol**i**ce
Θ θ thita	**th**ong	Φ φ fee	**f**end
I ι iota	p**i**ck	X χ hee	lo**ch**
K κ kappa	**k**ind	Ψ ψ psee	syna**pse**
Λ λ lamda	**l**ink	Ω ω omega	**o**n (or owe
M μ mee	**m**other		at the end
N ν nee	**n**ice		of words)

There are numerous letter combinations that make unpredictable sounds but this is rather off-putting for the beginner and so if you think you are ready for them, it is time to buy a teach yourself book.

Some conversational gambits

Meanwhile, it is useful to be able to form a few elementary questions and make one or two simple statements. Apart from ensuring your basic survival and comfort when there is no one around who speaks English this will, as said before, create a really friendly rapport with the local people.

The following lists will help you to put a few simple sentences together. Of course, these will not be in grammatically perfect Greek (a language cannot be learned so easily) but if you say them carefully they should be comprehensible to any Greek person, who will be absolutely delighted by the effort you have made. Remember to stress the accented syllables.

List A — basic statements and phrases

Yes: *neh*
No: *óhee*
Please/you are welcome: *parra kallóh*
Thank you: *efharistóe*
Good morning: *kallee máira*
Good evening: *kallee spáira*
Good night: *kallee níhta*
Hello/goodbye: *Yássoo* (*yássas* is more formal)
Greetings: *hyéretay*
Where is: *poo eénay*

I want: *thélloh*
I am: *éemay*
You are: *éesthay*
He/she is/there is/they are: *eenay*
We are: *ee már stay*
I have: *éhoe*
You have: *éhetay*
He/she/it has: *éhee*
We have: *éhoomay*
They have: *éhoon*
I don't want: *then thélloh*

Now if you turn to lists B, C and D you can add words to some of these to articulate your needs or ideas. Statements can be turned into questions by putting an intonation in your voice — to change "you are" to "are you?", for instance

List B — accommodation

hotel: *ksennoe doheé oh*
room: *thomátteeoh*
house: *spéetee*
bathroom: *bányoh*
shower: *dóos*

bed: *krevártee*
hot: *zéstee*
cold: *kréeoh*
blanket: *koo vérta*

List C — getting about

far: *makree áre*
near: *kondá*
bus: *leo for éeoh*
taxi: *taxí*
ferry boat: *férry bott*
street: *óh thos*
road: *dróh moss*
corner: *go neár*
left: *arist erráh*

right: *thex ee áh*
single: *applóh*
return: *epist rofée*
ticket: *ee sit ée ree ah*
post office: *tahee droh mée oh*
laundry: *plind éereeoh*
bank: *tráp ezza*
telephone: *telléfonoh*
petrol: *vrin zée nee*

List D — eating and drinking

restaurant: *eest ee at
  ór ee oh*
food: *figh eet óh*
coffee: *kaféh*
tea: *ts ígh*
breakfast: *proh ee nóh*
sugar: *záh harree*

salt: *a lár tee*
pepper: *pip áir ee*
wine: *krass ée*
beer: *béerah*
water: *nair óh*
without: *hórris*
oil: *lárthee*

List E — other useful phrases and words

As you gain a little confidence — and begin to understand the replies you get — you will probably be able to make use of the following phrases and words — when shopping, for instance. Note that, although days and numbers have been given here, it is more difficult to talk about time, such as the hours of boats and buses, so that is when you ask for it to be written down!

  I want this: *thélloh aftóh*
  I don't want this: *then thélloh aftóh*
  What time does it leave?: *tee óra févyee*

What time does it arrive?: *tee óra ftáhnee*
Please write it down: *moo toh gráps etay parra kallóh*
Excuse me/sorry: *sig nóh mee*
I am an Englishman/woman: *éemay ángloss/angléeda*
Please speak slowly: *méelet ay argár parra kallóh*
Don't!: *mee!*
Go away!: féev yet ay!
Help!: *voh ée thee ah!*

Monday: theftéra
Tuesday: *tréetee*
Wednesday: *tetártee*
Thursday: *pémptee*
Friday: *parraskevée*
Saturday: *sávatoh*
Sunday: *kiree akée*

one: énna
two: *thé oh*
three: *trée ya*
four: *téssera*
five: *pénday*
six: *éxee*
seven: *eptá*
eight: *oktoé*
nine: *enay yáh*
ten: *théka*
eleven: *én theka*
twelve: *thó theka*
twenty: *ée cosee*
thirty: *tree ánda*
forty: *sarránda*

fifty: *penninda*
sixty: *ex índa*
seventy: *ev tho mínda*
eighty: *ovthónda*
ninety: *en en índa*
one hundred: *eka tón*
two hundred: *thee ak ówsee ah*
three hundred: *track ówsee ah*
four hundred: *tétrak oswee ah*
five hundred: *pént ak owsee ah*
seven hundred: *eptak ówsee ah*
eight hundred: *okt ak ówsee ah*
nine hundred: *enyak ówsee ah*
thousand: *hill eeyá*

Appendix B
Wind Force: The Beaufort Scale*

B'Fort No.	Wind Descrip.	Effect on land	Effect on sea	Wind Speed			Wave height (m)¼
				knots	mph	kph	
0	Calm	Smoke rises vertically	Sea like a mirror	less than 1			-
1	Light air	Direction shown by smoke but not by wind vane	Ripples with appearance of scales; no foam crests	1-3	1-3	1-2	-
2	Light breeze	Wind felt on face; leaves rustle; wind vanes move	Small wavelets; crests do not break	4-6	4-7	6-11	0.15-0.30
3	Gentle breeze	Leaves and twigs in motion wind extends light flag	Large wavelets; crests begin to break; scattered white horses	7-10	8-12	13-19	0.60-1.00
4	Moderate breeze	Small branches move; dust and loose paper raised	Small waves, becoming longer; fairly frequent white horses	11-16	13-18	21-29	1.00-1.50
5	Fresh breeze	Small trees in leaf begin to sway	Moderate waves; many white horses; chance of some spray	17-21	19-24	30-38	1.80-2.50
6	Strong breeze	Large branches in motion; telegraph wires whistle	Large waves begin to form; white crests extensive; some	22-27	25-31	40-50	3.00-4.00

7	Near gale	Whole trees in motion; difficult to walk against wind	Sea heaps up; white foam from breaking waves begins to be blown in streaks	28-33	32-38	51-61	4.00-6.00
8	Gale	Twigs break off trees; progress impeded	Moderately high waves; foam blown in well-marked streaks	34-40	39-46	63-74	5.50-7.50
9	Strong gale	Chimney pots and slates blown off	High waves; dense streaks of foam; wave crests begin to roll over; heavy spray	41-47	47-54	75-86	7.00-9.75
10	Storm	Trees uprooted; considerable structural damage	Very high waves, overhanging crests; dense white foam streaks; sea takes on white appearance; visibility affected	48-56	66-63	88-100	9.00-12.50
11	Violent storm	Widespread damage, seldom experienced in England	Exceptionally high waves; dense patches of foam; wave crests blown into froth; visibility affected	57-65	64-75	101-110	11.30-16.00
12	Hurricane	Winds of this force encountered only in Tropics	Air filled with foam & spray; visibility seriously affected	65 +	75 +	120 +	13.70 +

* Introduced in 1805 by Sir Francis Beaufort (1774-1857) hydrographer to the Navy

¼ First figure indicates average height of waves; second figure indicates maximum height.

Appendix C

Useful conversion tables

Distance/Height

feet	ft or m	metres
3.281	1	0.305
6.562	2	0.610
9.843	3	0.914
13.123	4	1.219
16.404	5	1.524
19.685	6	8.829
22.966	7	2.134
26.247	8	2.438
29.528	9	2.743
32.808	10	3.048
65.617	20	8.096
82.081	25	7.620
164.05	50	15.25
328.1	100	30.5
3281.	1000	305.

Weight

pounds	kg or lb	kilograms
2.205	1	0.454
4.409	2	0.907
8.819	4	1.814
13.228	6	2.722
17.637	8	3.629
22.046	10	4.536
44.093	20	9.072
55.116	25	11.340
110.231	50	22.680
220.462	100	45.359

Distance

miles	km or mls	kilometres
0.621	1	1.609
1.243	2	3.219
1.864	3	4.828
2.486	4	6.437
3.107	5	8.047
3.728	6	9.656
4.350	7	11.265
4.971	8	12.875
5.592	9	14.484
6.214	10	16.093
12.428	20	32.186
15.534	25	40.234
31.069	50	80.467
62.13	100	160.93
621.3	1000	1609.3

Dress sizes

Size	bust/hip inches	bust/hip centimetres
8	30/32	76/81
10	32/34	81/86
12	34/36	86/91
14	36/38	91/97
16	38/40	97/102
18	40/42	102/107
20	42/44	107/112
22	44/46	112/117
24	46/48	117/112

Tyre pressure

lb per sq in	kg per sq cm
14	0.984
16	1.125
18	1.266
20	1.406
22	1.547
24	1.687
26	1.828
28	1.969
30	2.109
40	2.812

Temperature

centigrade	fahrenheit
0	32
5	41
10	50
20	68
30	86
40	104
50	122
60	140
70	158
80	176
90	194
100	212

Oven Temperatures

Electric	Gas mark	Centigrade
225	¼	110
250	½	130
275	1	140
300	2	150
325	3	170
350	4	180
375	5	190
400	6	200
425	7	220
450	8	230

Your weight in kilos

stones

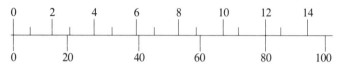

kilograms

Liquids

gallons	gal or l	litres
0.220	1	4.546
0.440	2	9.092
0.880	4	18.184
1.320	6	27.276
1.760	8	36.368
2.200	10	45,460
4.400	20	90.919
5.500	25	113.649
10.999	50	227.298
21.998	100	454.596

Some handy equivalents for self caterers

1 oz	25 g	1 fluid ounce	25 ml
4 oz	125 g	¼ pt. (1 gill)	142 ml
8 oz	250 g	½ pt.	284 ml
1 lb	500 g	¾ pt.	426 ml
2.2 lb	1 kilo	1 pt	568 ml
		1¾ pints	1 litre

INDEX

Abbreviations: (A) Antipaxos; (P) Paxos